Victims of Vanity

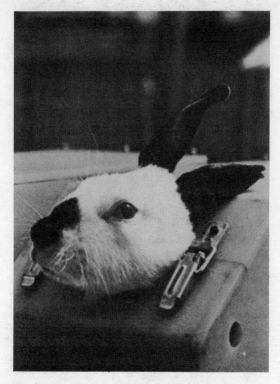

Ready for the Draize Eye Test
Credit: People for the Ethical Treatment of Animals

ANIMAL TESTING OF COSMETICS

AND HOUSEHOLD PRODUCTS

AND HOW TO STOP IT

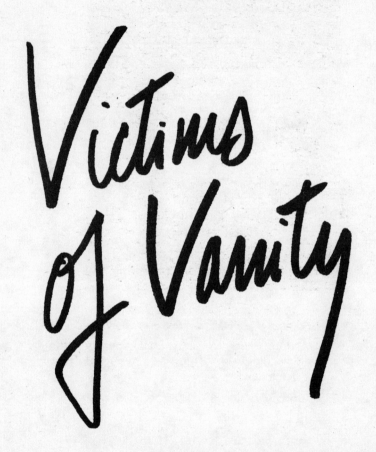

Victims of Vanity

LYNDA DICKINSON

SUMMERHILL PRESS, TORONTO

Published by Summerhill Press Ltd.
52 Shaftesbury Avenue
Toronto, Ontario M4T 1A2

Distributed in Canada by University of Toronto Press
5201 Dufferin Street
Downsview, Ontario M3H 5T8

Distrubuted in the United States by Sterling Publishing
387 Park Avenue South
New York, New York 10016-8810

Book design by Michelle Maynes
Cover photo courtesy of
Toronto Humane Society
Friends of Animals

Canadian Cataloguing in Publication Data
Dickinson, Lynda, 1959-
Victims of vanity

ISBN 0-920197-90-6

1. Toxicity testing — In vitro. 2. Animal experimentation.
3. Cosmetics — Toxicology — Testing. 4. Commercial products —
Toxicolology — Testing. I. Title.

HV4915.D52 1989   636.08'85   C89-094969-7

Printed and bound in Canada

This book is dedicated to:

Marcia Pearson, whose enlightenment and enthusiasm
have given me the necessary strength
to carry on...

Jeff, whose support and understanding
have gone above and beyond
the call of duty.

Deane. I love you, and always will.

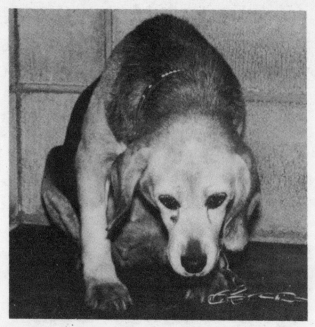

Day 6 of an LD50 acute toxicity test.
© Brian Gunn — IAAPEA

April 24

Today we will remember you.
A few diehards will chant and shout for the animals,
stoke the fires of change,
but a slow wind feeds this fire,
and tomorrow the rest of the world will forget.

A dog, maybe a monkey, only a rat —
someone unhuman, less than human, maybe even the
same —
cries in the dark
and cannot bear another moment of pain.
He dreams of a place called home
but waking remembers it is only a dream.

Yet maybe they will think of you
with the soap they use to wash away dirt
like sins they forget or choose to ignore,
with the powders and shadows they wear to hide truths,
or the polish they sweat over so their floors shine just so.
Yes, the rest of the world, in its way
does remember you but thinks nothing
of what you have given so they can have more.

Every day I remember you
and cry out to my God each night before sleep
when your face looks like mine
and the thought is too hard to bear.
What must I do?
What, then, must we do?

JUDY ALLEN-NEWBURY

April 24th marks the International Week of
Rememberance for Laboratory Animals

TABLE OF CONTENTS

ACKNOWLEGEMENTS

The research and preparation of this book involved the work, time, and assistance of a number of people, many of whom are now my friends. Special thanks to:
Margot Franssen
Dr. Ethel Thurston
JoAnne and Michael Schwab
Dr. Andrew Karp
Louis Tsao
Tita Zierer

FOREWORD

Even with all my own research and reading I still am amazed that there is so much to be learned about the use of animals in experimental research. *Victims of Vanity* pulls no punches and provides the reader with hard-hitting facts about the use of animals by companies in their attempt to prove cosmetics and household products safe for humans.

Lynda Dickinson, a former model and therefore a prime user and promoter of cosmetics through her work, has taken a close look at what is being used in the name of beauty and the cruelty that is hidden behind this facade.

One of the key objectives of any book should be to educate its readers, and that feat is accomplished here. Not only are the behind-the-scenes methods of experimentation explained, but the reader is given ways to help stop this animal abuse. In addition, there is a long list both of cruelty-free products and also of groups that are trying to stop cruelty to animals.

From the beginning of my work in animal rights, I have advocated the elimination of animal experimentation. Animals and humans are different, and results from tests done on one cannot be extrapolated to the other. Veterinarians will be the first to admit that a compound used on a dog may cause a completely different reaction when used on a cat because they are different species. The same applies to humans. This book describes some of these differences and also talks about alternatives.

Anyone who has heard me lecture knows that I am opposed to the word "alternative" since you can't have an alternative to something that doesn't work in the first place. In this book, however, the author has used "alternative" as a simplified term to represent true and proper research that is going on with tissue culture and computer modeling.

With the use of human tissue cultures and modern computers, the true scientist has emerged. Even among the many varieties of Homo Sapiens there are different reactions to various compounds, but at least the basic physiology is similar.

The reader's first reaction to the facts contained in this book might be disbelief that this kind of torture can go on in a civilized country such as ours. This is a good reaction since it alerts the reader to the existence of other areas of society that might also commit these "hidden crimes." We cannot allow our knowledge to be determined solely by what our governments and doctors tell us; we must instead, research the subject ourselves. In this regard, Lynda Dickinson's *Victims of Vanity* provides a most valuable resource.

Michael Schwab, BCS, MCS, CPA

Director, C-VAR (Canadian Vegans for Animal Rights)

Producer and host of "The Extended Circle",

a weekly animal rights radio show in Toronto

INTRODUCTION

> Animal tests are no guarantee of safety in humans. I know of no physician who relies on these tests in deciding treatment for cases of accidental poisoning.
>
> DAVID LEES, M.D., BETHESDA, MARYLAND

Lipstick, face cream, anti-perspirant, laundry detergent... these products and hundreds of other personal care and household items have one common ingredient: the suffering and death of millions of animals.

An average of 25 million animals die every year in North America for the testing of everything from new cosmetics to new methods of warfare. Five hundred thousand to one million of these animals are sacrificed each year to test new cosmetics alone. [1]

Of all the pain and suffering caused by animal research, cosmetic and household product testing is among the least justifiable, as it cannot even be argued that tests are done to improve the quality of human life.

Animals have doses of shampoo, hair spray, and deodorant dripped into their eyes or applied to bare skin in attempts to measure eye and skin irritancy levels. Others are force-fed massive quantities of toxic materials such as bleach or soap, in a hit-and-miss attempt to measure levels of toxicity.

Since 1938, The Food and Drug Administration (U.S.

---

[1] "Special Edition Copy," PETA News, (Washington, D.C.: [People for the Ethical Treatment of Animals], n.d.): 1.

13

FDA) has required that each ingredient in a cosmetic be "adequately substantiated for safety"[2] prior to being made available to the consumer. However, neither the FDA nor the Consumer Product Safety Commission (a regulatory agency that oversees product safety, consumer complaints, etc.) requires firms to conduct animal testing of any cosmetic product. Cosmetic companies use animal tests to insure themselves against possible consumer lawsuits. If sued for liability, they can protect themselves by arguing that the cosmetic was "adequately tested for safety" with tests standard in the cosmetic industry.

Due to recent minimal public pressure, a number of cosmetic companies, such as Revlon, Procter & Gamble, and Bristol-Myers, whose policy is to test their products on animals, have begun to set aside a percentage of their annual income to help finance research for alternative kinds of tests. However, the contribution is minute compared to the phenomenal cost of scientific research; therefore research has been both limited and brought periodically to a halt due to the lack of sufficient funding.

If research for alternatives to animal testing were as well-funded as research using animal tests, unlimited replacements to live animal subjects would soon be found. More public pressure is needed to convince major cosmetic companies to provide the money required to fund alternative methods of research to replace live animals.

Numerous companies such as Noxema and Estée Lauder, have repeatedly assured animal welfare groups that their laboratory animals receive "the best of care and treatment" and are in no way subjected to cruelty and inhumanity. However, despite their development of humane guidelines for animal testing, the number of animals used in tests and

---

[2.] United States of America, *Code of Federal Regulations*, Title 21. (Washington, D.C.) Parts 600 to 799.

experiments continues to grow at an alarming rate. A total of over 20 million animals were used in North American laboratories in 1986. That figure rose by another 5 percent in 1987, and again in 1988.

In the United Kingdom over 16,000 animals died in cosmetic and related product testing in 1985, and nearly 10,000 died in the testing of household products. Again, these figures rose by another 5 to 7 percent a year in 1986, 1987, and 1988.[3]

The small number of companies such as Rachel Perry that have recently changed their testing practices from live animals to alternative methods have done so as a direct response to pressure from animal welfare groups and the general consumer, presumably in fear of declining sales of their products.

Canada has no legislation to protect laboratory animals from any form of mistreatment, abuse, or neglect. Great Britain has nothing in the way of constitutional ethical treatment of laboratory animals. In the United States, the U.S. Welfare Animal Act (passed in 1966 and later amended in 1970 and 1976) charges the U.S. Department of Agriculture with overseeing the humane handling and housing of animals in laboratories, pet dealerships, and exhibitions. While the law covers lab animals (such as rabbits, mice, dogs, and monkeys) it does not state that the animals are to be cared for or to be treated for injuries received from experiments, nor does it state that animals in laboratories can be used for only a limited number of experiments with the least possible suffering and distress. In effect then, there is no protection given to lab animals.

Regardless of its species, if an animal is to be used for an experiment, it is considered a "tool" and nothing more. Experimenters in all countries are free to do with it as they please.

[3.] "How Animals Suffer," *Choose Cruelty-Free* Spring/Summer 1987: 3.

The tests are crude, cruel, and unreliable. Animals injured in acute toxicity and eye irritancy tests are never treated. If the animals do not die from the effects of the experiment itself, they are either killed for an autopsy, or, if they are not badly injured, recycled and used for additional tests.

Since the animals are not treated, these tests provide little useful knowledge for the treatment of humans who are exposed to the harmful substances. Dr. Gil Langley, a scientific neuro-chemist, states that: "Results [of animal tests] vary dramatically from laboratory to laboratory, between strains, sex, age, and species of animals, and extrapolation to humans is questionable."

Animal tests have failed to provide the clear definition between *harmful* and *harmless* products that they were originally intended to provide. The cosmetic industry is the only industry that conducts animal toxicity tests that are *not required by law.*

Cosmetics are very low in toxic substances, and the most common consumer complaints to the manufacturers are allergic reactions, which animal testing *cannot* predict. Cosmetics that claim to be "allergy safe" are usually products that contain little or no fragrance, reduced amounts of oils, and added natural ingredients such as aloe, or other plant extracts; they are usually tested by human volunteers. Therefore, regardless of animal testing, the consumer always becomes the so-called "guinea pig" for any new product. It would then benefit the consumer to have up-to-date scientific methods, rather than the outdated, unreliable processes using laboratory animals.

Victims of Vanity will take you behind the glossy packaging, media-magic, and razzle-dazzle world of cosmetic advertising, to view a grim and grisly world where millions of animals are blinded, poisoned, and suffocated to test a "new" shade of eyeshadow, or a "new and improved" dish soap. This book will tell you why animal tests are outdated and unnecessary, and why testing a product in a rabbit's eye does not assure product safety for human beings.

Victims of Vanity will also tell you about the scientific alternatives available, and how they not only preserve the lives and dignity of animals, but can also ensure the consumer of product safety.

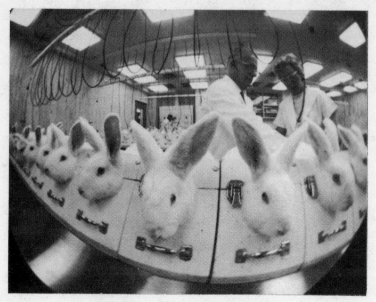

Rabbits ready for Draize Eye Test
Credit: People for the Ethical Treatment of Animals Inc.

Chapter 1

ANIMAL TESTS: POINTLESS TORTURE

THE DRAIZE TEST

> I consider the Draize test archaic, cruel, irrational and dangerous, and the rationale for its use has nothing to do with human welfare.
>
> DR. MURRAY COHEN, ASSISTANT PROFESSOR OF CLINICAL PSYCHIATRY, MOUNT SINAI MEDICAL CENTER, NEW YORK, NY

The Draize Eye Irritancy Test, developed by Dr. John Draize in 1944, is the standard test for irritation and tissue damage of products that might get into the human eye. These products range from eye shadow, shampoos, and detergents to the most caustic of household products. This test is responsible for the suffering of thousands of white albino rabbits every year.

Rabbits are chosen for this test because their eyes are far more sensitive than those of any other animals, including the human, and therefore their capacity for irritation is much greater. Their tear ducts are not as well developed and efficient as those of humans, so they cannot produce enough tears to wash away irritants that are placed into their eyes. Albino rabbits are used because they have very little eye pigment, so irritation, ulceration, inflammation, and tissue damage caused to the eye can be easily seen.

Between 6 to 18 rabbits are restrained in stocks from which only their heads protrude. The restraints prevent the animals from scratching their eyes or shaking their heads to dislodge the substance.

The lower lid of one of the animal's eye is pulled away from the eyeball to form a tiny cup. Liquid, flake, granule, or powder substance is sprayed or placed into the cupped eye, while the other eye is left alone for comparison purposes. The reaction of the eye to the irritants is recorded every twenty-four hours for seven consecutive days.

During this time the rabbits suffer from extreme burning, swelling, hemorrhaging, and massive laceration of the iris. Sight is eventually lost in the experimental eye. Anaesthesia or pain-relieving drugs are not administered lest the drugs interfere with test results. Rabbits have been known to scream or to break their necks in severe but futile struggles to escape the pain and agony.

VALIDITY OF THE DRAIZE TEST

Since the rabbit's eye has a thinner cornea and is more sensitive and reactive to substances than the human eye, scientists such as Dr. Stephen Kaufman, ophthalmologist at the New York University Department of Ophthalmology, believe that results of the tests done on rabbits' eyes bear little connection to the effect a substance would have on a human eye. The structural differences do not allow for valid comparison.

Dr. Neal Barnard, M.D., physician at the George Washington University School of Medicine, and Head of the

After the Draize Eye Test
Credit: Toronto Humane Society/Ark II

Physician's Committee for Responsible Medicine, Washington, D.C., states that "the Draize test is an archaic measure of eye irritancy. It is also a highly subjective test which may be read differently by different observers." What may be described as "red and inflamed" by one observer may look "pink and irritated " to another. Therefore, not only do test results not necessarily apply to humans, but they are also in themselves inconsistent and inaccurate in determining degrees of irritation.

A major test conducted by Carrol S. Weil and Robert A. Scala (1971) of the Carnegie University of Pittsburgh, in collaboration with Esso Research and Engineering Company, proved the unreliability of the Draize test. Substances were distributed to 24 laboratories for testing purposes. Not only did the results show extreme variations in the way the

21

laboratories evaluated the rabbit's reaction, but while certain labs recorded unusually "severe" reactions to the substances, others concluded the substance to be "non-irritating".

This study concluded that "the [Draize] test should not be recommended as the standard procedure in any new regulation."[4]

THE LETHAL DOSE 50 PERCENT TEST

> The [LD50] test is a ritual slaughter which has no useful meaning.
>
> DR. ROBERT SHARPE, PH.D., FORMER SENIOR RESEARCH FELLOW AT THE ROYAL POSTGRADUATE MEDICAL SCHOOL, ENGLAND

> I do not think the LD50 test provides much useful information about the health hazards to humans from chemicals...the National Toxicology Program does not use the LD50.
>
> DR. DAVID, DIRECTOR OF THE NATIONAL TOXICOLOGY PROGRAM, U.S.A.

LD50 stands for Lethal Dose 50 percent, a name resulting from the test's intent to estimate the amount of a substance required to kill 50 percent of a group of laboratory test animals, such as rats, mice, guinea pigs, monkeys, pigs, and dogs.

The test was originally developed in 1927 by J.W. Trevan, an English mathematician, to estimate the poisonous potentials of very potent drugs. Over time, it became routinely incorporated by cosmetic and product companies, to test various chemical compounds designed for human use in North America and abroad.

---

[4] C.S. Weil and R.A. Scala, "Study of Intra and Interlaboratory Variability in the Results of Rabbit Eye and Skin Irritation Tests," *Toxicology and Applied Pharmacology* 19: 276–360, 1971, as quoted in "Beyond the Draize Test," Physicians Committee for Responsible Medicine (Washington, D.C.: [PCRM], n.d.): 10.

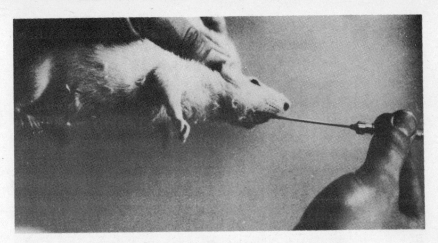

Administering the Lethal Dose 50 Percent Test
Credit: BUAV, U.K.

Compounds that constitute products such as lipstick, face powder, nail polish, hair dye, creams and lotions, bleach, and laundry detergent, as well as the finished product itself, are routinely tested with the LD50 test.

All "new" products, as well as chemicals and compounds that are added to "new and improved" products, are also tested for toxicity, using one or several variations of the LD50 test. Listed below are descriptions of the various LD50 tests.

Acute Toxicity Test
The Acute Toxicity Test requires between 60 to 100 animals to determine what constitutes a lethal dose of a particular substance. The test spans a time period from two weeks to seven years, depending on the amount of toxic chemicals in the product being tested. The animals are observed daily. Since chemicals are bitter-tasting and have an unpleasant smell, animals refuse to swallow them. The animals are then forced to swallow the substances in the form of capsules or pellets. They are also force-fed liquid chemicals by stomach tube, or through a hole cut in the animal's throat.

Some animals die from the sheer bulk of the dosage

23

administered or from the severe burns they receive in the throat and stomach from the chemicals used in products such as laundry bleach and detergent, mildew remover, liquid drain cleaner, aftershave, and cologne.

In addition to attempting to record what constitutes a lethal amount, the experimenters record the time, duration and severity of the attack caused by the poison. The reaction of the pupils, pulse, respiration, and general behaviour of the animals are also noted.

Loss of appetite, excessive defecation, gasping, vomiting, bleeding from the eyes, nose and mouth, severe convulsions, and paralysis are some of the symptoms the animals display after massive doses of chemicals block and rupture their internal organs.

The 50 percent of the animals that survive the test period, are subsequently killed and dissected so that their organs can

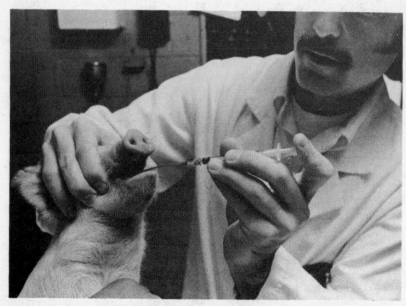

Forcefeeding for the Acute Toxicity Test
Credit: Toronto Humane Society

The environment and the effect of the Acute Toxicity Test
Credit BUAV, U.K.

be examined and analyzed. The information is stored for studies of statistical determination of toxicity.

Sub-Acute Toxicity Test

Like the Acute Test, this test also calls for the substance to be administered orally, and again, because of the bitter taste and strong, unpleasant smell, the animals refuse to swallow it. Powder, pellets, or liquid substance is forced into the animals by means of a stomach tube, or by oral injections to the stomach.

The same reactions occur in the animals of this test as those of the Acute Test, and again, at the end of the allocated time period, those animals that survive are killed so their tissue and organs can be examined for the effects of the chemicals.

The major differences between the Acute Toxicity Test and the Sub-Acute Toxicity Test are the duration of the tests and the observation period of the laboratory animals. The

25

maximum duration of the Sub-Acute Test is a 90-day period, and observation of the animals occurs usually only every other day, rather than every day.

Acute Dermal Toxicity Test

The purpose of the Acute Dermal Toxicity Test is to determine the daily degree of skin irritation for the allocated test period. Mice, guinea pigs, rabbits and dogs are used.

To administer the test, a large patch of skin on one side of the animal is smoothly shaved and abrasions made with a sharp surgical instrument or hypodermic needle. Substances such as deodorant, talcum powder, or abrasive household cleaners are directly applied to the abraded skin. Gauze is then wrapped around the animal's body to secure in place the test material. A rubber sleeve is positioned to fit snugly around the animal's trunk. The animals are either immobilized in a multiple animal holder or have a large plastic collar fastened around their necks to prevent them from chewing at the sleeve.

Exposure of the skin to the substance continues for up to twenty-four hours. As the poison invades their system, most animals suffer from blistered and burned skin, vomiting, convulsions, and coma.

Incidents have been recorded of rabbits found with their paws caught in the collar, and the animal near death from asphyxiation. Death has also resulted from eating the plastic sleeve and gauze which subsequently lodged in the animal's intestines and blocked the flow of faeces.[5]

Chronic Toxicity Test

The aim of the Chronic Toxicity Test is to determine if a small dosage of a given substance, such as laundry bleach, might

---

[5] Leslie Fain, former Gillette employee, letter to International Animal Rights Cooperative, (Washington, D.C.: [IARC], 1987).

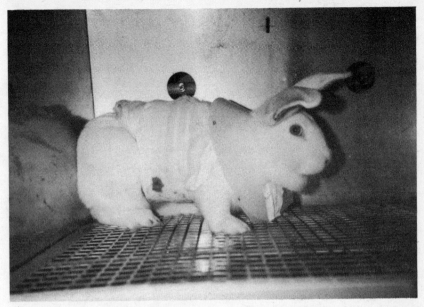

During the Acute Dermal Toxicity Test
Credit Toronto Humane Society/Ark II

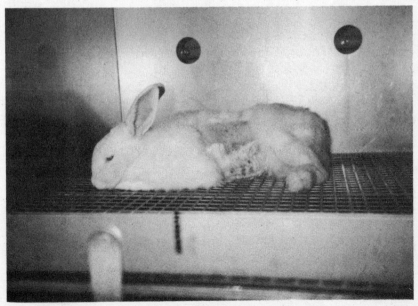

After the Acute Dermal Toxicity Test
Credit Toronto Humane Society/Ark II

have a poisonous effect if continuously ingested over a prolonged period of time. It is carried out on dogs, rats and rabbits. For rats and rabbits, the time allowed for this test is usually two years; for dogs, it is up to 7.

If the test animals refuse to consume the substance, they are force-fed through a stomach tube or by oral injections.

All animals do in fact become very ill, some actually dying and lingering near death for the duration of the test.

When the test is over, the surviving animals are then killed and their organs and tissues examined for the effects of the poisonous substances on their system.

Results are then stored for statistical purposes.

Acute Inhalation Test
The Acute Inhalation Test records the respiratory effects of long-term exposure to aerosol preparations such as hair spray, spray deodorant, spray room deodorizer, spray oven cleaner, and spray disinfectant.

Animals used in this test are rabbits, rats, guinea pigs, cats, and dogs.

The animals are confined, and often immobilized, in exposure chambers for a four-day period. They are sprayed around the head and upper part of the trunk for a specific period, usually 30 seconds, and left in the chamber for 15 minutes. The procedure is repeated every 30 minutes, until a total of 10 sprayings have been completed, therefore subjecting the animals to a total of 5 minutes of spraying and 2-1/2 hours in the sprayed chamber each day.

All animals suffer from nausea, shortness of breath, convulsions, coma, and some do not survive the test period at all. After being observed for the four-day period, the surviving animals are killed and their tissues examined for aerosol poisoning.

Sub-Acute Inhalation Test
The Sub-Acute Inhalation Test varies from the Acute Test in intensity and duration. In the Sub-Acute Test, animals are

Sub-Acute Inhalation Test
Credit: BUAV, UK

subjected to 2 30-second continuous sprayings daily, for a 90-day period. The animals used in this test are rabbits, guinea pigs, rats, cats, and dogs.

After reactions similar to those of the Acute Inhalation Test, the surviving animals are killed so their organs and tissues can be studied for the effects of the aerosol sprays.

VALIDITY OF THE LETHAL DOSE 50 PERCENT TEST

> ...for the determination of the human lethal dose, the LD50 test in animals is of very little value.
>
> DR. GERHARDT ZBINDER,
> SWISS TOXICOLOGIST

It has been known for over 20 years, by animal researchers and animal activists alike, that most scientists and toxicologists around the world have lost any respect they might once

29

have had for the validity of the LD50 tests. The tests have been criticized for their inhumanity, and for the irrelevance to humans of the data they produce.[6]

The results gained from this procedure are that a specific amount of a product has a 50 percent chance of killing a rabbit, mouse or dog. However, to be of any use to humans, the test would need to give the *exact* amount of the substance required to poison a human, which the LD50 test, or any other animal test, does *not* do.

Dr. Neal D. Barnard of George Washington University School of Medicine states that: "never in my years of training and practice have I seen any physician change the treatment strategy based on the LD50 or any other toxicity testing data. Rather, of paramount importance is the knowledge of the chemical make-up of the ingested compound which is derived from antidote which is appropriate to neutralize the effects of the ingested substance."[7]

It has been estimated that with animal subjects only about 25 percent of the side effects can be recorded, as animals cannot reveal symptoms such as headache, nausea, dizziness, light-headedness, cramps, and ringing of the ears. It is therefore easy to understand that due to physical, anatomical, and metabolical differences between human beings and animals, the LD50 tests fail to provide either consistent results, or useful information in areas of great concern, such as:

- the exact poisonous dose of a substance
- the prevention or correction of an overdose

[6.] "Fact Sheet: Classical LD50 Acute Toxicity Test," The Humane Society of the United States, (Washington, D.C.: [HSUS], June, 1988).

[7.] Dr. Neal D. Barnard, M.D., Chairman, PCRM, "The Maryland Cosmetics and Household Products Testing Bill: An Information Packet for Animal Welfare Activists" (Silverspring, Maryland: [Maryland Legislation for Animal Welfare], 1988).

- poisonous risks to newborns and infants (most test animals are adults, in excess of two years of age, whereas most *accidental* poisonings occur in children under the age of five)
- the harmful and non-harmful dose of any given substance
- the long-term effects of a substance in the human body
- which organs are specifically affected by any given dose.[8]

Practically anything in excess can be fatally harmful. Because most cosmetics are non-toxic, enormous quantities have to be fed to the test animals in order to cause death in 50 percent of them. With all LD50 percent tests, the dosage of toxic materials must be adjusted to kill 50 percent of the test animals.[9] In many cases, the deaths result because of the massive doses that block internal organs, and not because the substance being tested is in itself poisonous.

Even when an LD50 test shows that a substance is "safe" for laboratory animals, it means little for humans, as "it is...rarely possible to extrapolate from the LD50 in animals, to the lethal dose in man."[10]

FACTORS AFFECTING TEST RESULTS
The following unavoidable factors can affect test results:

- Stress: The animal's unnatural surroundings and routine laboratory activities can cause adverse effects quite apart from those of the experiment.
- Age: Test results can vary even if performed on the same species, if the animals' ages differ.

---

[8] "Newsletter," HSUS, June 1988.

[9] *PETA Fact Sheet*, n.d.

[10] G. Zbinder and M. Flurry-Roservi, *Archives in Toxicology*, 1981, as quoted by Neal D. Barnard, "Newsletter," PCRM, n.d.

- Diet: Results can vary between an animal that is still able to eat during the time of the experiment and an animal that is unable to eat or drink.

- Gender: Data variation has been known to differ between male and female laboratory animals of the same species.

- Isolation: Most animals routinely used in laboratory experiments are social pack animals, and have a need to be in a social environment with their own species. Research studies have shown that not only does isolation affect the animal's psychological behaviour but, in species such as mice, laboratory confinement also eliminates their need for self-grooming, a function that controls skin infections.[11]

- Crowding: Crowding has been proven to affect the animal's normal characteristic make-up, as it hinders physical development and tolerance to disease and parasites, and interrupts normal dietary behaviour.

While it is easy to note that numerous factors are responsible for causing physical and psychological conditions and alterations to character in laboratory animals, it is very difficult to assess the degree to which the animals are affected or the degree to which these alterations affect data generated in routine product testing.

[11.] Fraser and Waddell, 1974 studies, as cited in "Newsletter," HSUS, n.d.

Chapter 2

COMPANIES THAT CONDUCT ANIMAL TESTING

Though the following cosmetic and product companies have local and regional offices in Canada and in the United Kingdom, the addresses given on the following pages are the addresses of the head offices. Decisions made at headquarters affect the local and regional branches world-wide.

Companies marked with an asterisk have announced that they have discontinued animal testing. They remain on this list, however, because they are unable to guarantee that their product ingredients are not tested on animals by their suppliers. While their efforts to eliminate animal testing are commendable, these companies do not yet qualify as cruelty-free.

This list was compiled with the assistance of People for the Ethical Treatment of Animals, Washington, DC.

ALBERTO-CULVER CO.
2525 Armitage Avenue
Melrose Park, Illinois
60160

ALMAY
850 - 3rd Avenue
New York, New York
10022

AMERICAN CYANAMID CO.
697 Route 46
Clifton, New Jersey
07015

AMWAY CORP. *
7575 East Fulton Road
Ada, Michigan
49355-0001

ARAMIS, INC.
767 - 5th Avenue
New York, New York
10153

ARMOUR-DIAL INC.
Greyhound Tower
Phoenix, Arizona
85077

 AVON PRODUCTS, INC. *
9 West 57th Street
New York, New York
10019

BEECHAM COSMETICS, INC.
600 Eagle Drive
Bensenville, Illinois
60106-1977

BONNE BELL, INC.
Georgetown Row
Lakewood, Ohio
44107

BOYLE-MIDWAY
685 - 3rd Avenue
New York, New York
10017

BRECK
697 Route 46
Clifton, New Jersey
07015

BRISTON-MYERS CO.
345 Park Avenue
New York, New York
10022

CHANEL, INC.
9 West 57th Street
New York, New York
10019

CHARLES OF THE RITZ GROUP LTD.
770 Broadway
New York, New York
10003

CHEESEBROUGH-PONDS, INC.
33 Benedict Place
Greenwich, Connecticut
06830

CHRISTIAN DIOR PERFUMES
9 West 57th Street
New York, New York
10019

CLAIROL, INC.
345 Park Avenue
New York, New York
10154

CLARINS
540 Madison Avenue
New York, New York
10022

CLINIQUE LABORATORIES, INC.
767 - 5th Avenue
New York, New York
10153

CLOROX CO.
1221 Broadway
Oakland, California
94612

COLGATE-PALMOLIVE CO.
300 Park Avenue
New York, New York
10022

COSMAIR, INC.
PO Box 98
Westfield, New Jersey
07091

COTY
235 East 42nd Street
New York, New York
10017

DANA PERFUMES CORP.
609 - 5th Avenue
New York, New York
10017

DEL LABORATORIES
565 Broad Hollow Road
Farmingdale, New York
11735

DOROTHY GRAY
225 Summit Avenue
Montvale, New Jersey
07645

DOW CHEMICAL CO.
PO Box 68511
Indianapolis, Indiana
46268

ELIZABETH ARDEN
307 East McArty Street
Indianapolis, Indiana
46285

ESTEE LAUDER, INC.
767 - 5th Avenue
New York, New York
10153

FABERGE, INC. *
135 West 50th Street
New York, New York
10020

GERMAIN MONTEIL COSMETIQUE CORP.
40 West 57th Street
New York, New York
10019

GILLETTE CO.
PO Box 61
Boston, Massachusetts
02199

HELENA RUBENSTEIN
55 Hartz Way
Secaucus, New Jersey
07094

HELENA CURTIS INDUSTRIES, INC.
4401 West North Avenue
Chicago, Illinois
60639

HOUBIGANT, INC.
1135 Pleasant View Terrace
Ridgefield, New Jersey
07657-0299

JEAN PATOU, INC.
720 - 5th Avenue
New York, New York
10019

JERGENS
PO Box 145444
Cincinnati, Ohio
45214

JOHNSON & JOHNSON
1 Johnson & Johnson Plaza
New Brunswick, New Jersey
08933

JOHNSON PRODUCTS CO.,
INC.
8522 South Lafayette Avenue
Chicago, Illinois
60620

S. C. JOHNSON & SON INC.
1525 Howe Street
Racine, Wisconsin
53403-5011

JOVAN, INC.
875 North Michigan Avenue
Chicago, Illinois
60611

 LANCOME
530 - 5th Avenue
New York, New York
10036

LEVER BROTHERS CO.
390 Park Avenue
New York, New York
10022

L'OREAL
222 Terminal Avenue
Clarks, New Jersey
07066

MARY KAY COSMETICS,
INC. *
1330 Regal Row
Dallas, Texas
75247

MAX FACTOR & CO.
PO Box 728
Paramus, New Jersey
07652

MENNEN CO.
Hanover Avenue
Morristown, New Jersey
07960

 MERLE NORMAN
COSMETICS
15180 Bledsoe Street
Sylmar, California
91342

NEUTROGENA
5755 West 96th Street
Los Angeles, California
90045

NINA RICCI
697 Route 46
Clifton, New Jersey
07015

NORTON SIMMON INC.
277 Park Avenue
New York, New York
10017

NOXELL CORP. (COVER
GIRL COSMETICS)
Box 1799
Baltimore, Maryland
21203

PFIZER
235 East 42nd Street
New York, New York
10017

PROCTER AND GAMBLE CO.,
PO Box 599
Cincinnati, Ohio
45201

PUREX CORP.
5101 Clark Avenue
Lakewood, California
90712

REDKEN LABORATORIES, INC.
6625 Variel Avenue
Canoga Park, California
91303-2851

REVLON, INC. *
767 - 5th Avenue
New York, New York
10153

SCHERING-PLOUGH (MAYBELLINE COSMETICS)
Galloping Hill Road
Kenilworth, New Jersey
07033

SEA & SKI CORP.
1500 Spring Garden
Philadelphia, Pennsylvania
19101

SHAKLEE CORP.
444 Market Street
San Francisco, California
94111

SHISEDO COSMETICS
540 Madison Avenue
New York, New York
10022

SQUIBB
Route 35
Holmdel, New Jersey
07733

STERLING DRUG, INC.
90 Park Avenue
New York, New York
10016

SYNTEX
Box 170
Pierces Road
Newburgh, New York
12550

TEXIZE
Box 368
Greenville, South Carolina
29602

VIDAL SASSOON, INC.
Los Angeles, California
90067

WARNER-LAMBERT CO.
201 Tabor Road
Morris Plains, New York
07950

WELLA CORP.
525 Grand Avenue
Englewood, New Jersey
07631

* Documented Proof Of Switchover

Chapter 3

THE ALTERNATIVES: MAKING TODAY THE FUTURE

...in the case of the Draize Eye Test, test-tube techniques could provide a painless alternative today. Skin irritancy tests can, in many cases, be replaced by skin "patch" tests using human volunteers, a sensible choice already made by a number of companies. More severe irritants can be prescreened using cultures of skin tissues.

BRITISH UNION FOR THE ABOLITION OF
VIVISECTION, CHOOSE CRUELTY-FREE
NEWSLETTER, 1987

Numerous alternatives to replace animal testing methods are presently being researched in the United States, Canada, and Europe. Administrators of The Food and Drug Administration (U.S.) claim that the alternatives are just "potential replacement tests in various stages of evolution."[12]

In other words, the alternatives, many of which have

[12.] Frank E. Young, Commissioner of Food and Drugs, U.S.A., March 30, 1987, as quoted in a pamphlet from MLAW, September, 1987.

been in existence since 1985, have not yet been accepted as the "new " standard tests of the cosmetic industry. Most are still in pre-validation stages and may not be accepted by industry for several more years,[13] even though most yield information similar to or of greater value than the tests originally done on animals.

According to Dr. Sergey Fedoroff, Researcher, University of Saskatchewan, Saskatoon, Canada, "There are a number of alternatives to the Draize Test but they will not be accepted by the licencing agencies (Food and Drug Administration, Environmental Protection Agency, etc.) until industry begins to use them in its laboratories and demonstrates that the alternative tests are reproducible and reliable."

However, it seems that industry would prefer to pacify all those concerned with the cruelty of animal testing by offering a small portion of their profit (according to The United States Humane Society, about .01 percent of their annual income) to develop alternatives, rather that to sponsor further research for the purpose of validating already existing and developed alternatives.

In an attempt to reduce and eliminate animal suffering in research, scientists have developed a system of guidelines known as the *three R's* of alternatives; *replace* testing of animals with alternatives such as computer models and cell cultures; *refine* existing tests to lessen pain and suffering of the animals; and *reduce* the number of animals used in the experiments.

Replacing the animals with alternatives such as computer models and test tube methods would be not only humane but also cheaper and faster, with results reliably relevant to humans.

In the meantime, *refining* existing scientific methods of

[13.] "News Abstracts, Fall, 1987," The American Fund for Alternatives to Animal Research (New York, NY: [AFAAR] 1987): 1.

testing through the use of limited doses of pain killers and anaesthetics would lessen the stress, pain, and prolonged suffering of laboratory animals. There is no proof or recorded data to confirm the possibility that pain killers and anaesthetics interfere with test results.

While replacement tests are currently being modified and perfected, the number of animals routinely used could be drastically *reduced*. The traditional LD50 tests use up to 100 animals. New tests, which provide the same information, use no more than a total of 10 animals .

Funding for the research of alternatives to animal testing of cosmetics and household products is provided only by private sources. The governments of Canada, the United States and the United Kingdom have offered no public funds.

To date, the multi-billion dollar cosmetics, household products, pharmaceutical, pesticides, and chemical industries combined have contributed only about $6 million to the alternatives effort in North America and Britain. Yet these industries continue to use millions of animals to test their products.

The Cosmetics, Toiletry and Fragrance Association, a trade organization composed of about 500 organizational members, including some of the largest cosmetic companies in the United States, has contributed about $2.5 million. While grateful for the contribution, animal activists know the amount is not adequate to meet the high cost of scientific alternative research.[14] Not only is the research itself costly, but better funding is also required to attract the top scientists, who are currently in positions that offer better pay.

Incentive grants to help speed up the development, validation, and use of non-animal substitutes are being awarded

---

[14.] Carol Grunewald, "Are Companies Doing Enough to Stop Toxicity Testing on Animals?" The Animals' Agenda, September 1986: 17.

yearly by private sources such as The American Fund For Alternatives to Animal Research (AFAAR), by some cosmetic companies such as Revlon, and by some product companies such as Bristol-Myers, to the two centres for research of alternatives to animal testing in the United States: Rockefeller University and The Center for Alternatives to Animal Testing. But the lack of substantial funds is still the major obstacle to the successful development and validation of alternatives.

Replacement research could easily be sped up if the companies who use animal testing of their products would share in the funding of research to develop and validate alternatives. In addition, if some of the funds available for animal research were re-directed towards financing the development of *non-animal* research, the alternatives presented in the following section could be refined, validated, and incorporated as the "new" standard tests of the cosmetic industry, to reduce, if not end, the inhumane treatment of animals in laboratories.

DESCRIPTION OF THE TESTS
While there are many alternatives to animal testing being developed, the following list describes the most promising.

In-Vitro Alternatives

(Glass test-tube and culture-dish studies)

> ...discrimination among various degrees of irritation is a distinct advantage of *in-vitro* tests over animal tests.... And the Draize Test does not adequately reflect the degree of irritancy in humans.
>
> JOHNS HOPKINS MEDICAL INSTITUTION,
> NEWS RELEASE, APRIL 14, 1986

Not only is the Draize Test a poor way to treat animals, but the *in-vitro* method appears to be far more sensitive and far more relevant.

ARTHUR H. NEUFELD, PH.D.,
THE EYE RESEARCH INSTITUTE, BOSTON, MASS.

Single and Multiple Cell Cultures

Cell specimens taken directly from a human, during surgical operations, autopsies, and biopsies and from placentas, or animal organ tissue from abattoirs are kept alive in glass culture dishes in specifically prepared laboratory nutrients and additives.

As each generation of cells reproduces identical cells, there is no limit to the availability of standard test material. In addition, since the cells used in the tests are identical, final results are consistent, unlike in live animal tests where results vary according to the various factors affecting the individual animals.

Cell culture tests allow immediate observation of reactions to toxins, such as changes in permeability and metabolic activity, damage to genetic material, or cell death.[15] This is another advantage over animal tests where animals must be killed and dissected before the effects of toxic substances on their cells can be observed.

Organ Culture

I don't see any justification today for resorting to such tests [Draize and LD50]. The information can be readily obtained using assays and cultures.

DR. RICHARD SAN, CHIEF OF THE CARCINOGEN
TESTING LABORATORY, BRITISH COLUMBIA
CANCER RESEARCH CENTRE, VANCOUVER, B.C.

---

[15] "Congress of the United States Office of Technology Assessment" as quoted in a newsletter from Alternatives to Animal Use in Research, Testing and Education, (Washington, D.C.: [AAURTE], 1986).

Organ Culture involves taking single cells from an organ and allowing them to live and grow in laboratory solutions. Through cell regrowth, the original structure of the organ is retained, thus allowing the effects of a substance on an organ to be observed. The organ culture test yields the same results as those of a test done on a whole organ in an intact body.

As organs do not reproduce by natural process or have a long life span, an animal must be killed every time cultures are prepared. However, this killing can be done humanely and would not be preceded by the prolonged suffering of the traditional experiments. Also, thousands of organ cultures can be received from one animal, thus drastically reducing the number of animals needed.[16]

Both tissue and cell cultures can be frozen, stored, and thawed when required for use. Thanks to its flexibility and reliability, this method is used in biochemistry, cancer research, genetics, immunology, pharmacology, toxicology, nuclear medicine, and the production of vaccines. It could and should also be utilized for cosmetic testing.[17]

Eytex Screen

> ...the Eytex method for Draize...could dramatically reduce animal testing, resulting in large cost reductions while providing full and complete safety assurance.
>
> DR. CHRISTOPHER P. KELLY, CHAIRMAN,
> NATIONAL TESTING CORPORATION,
> PALM SPRINGS, CALIFORNIA

In 1982, Dr. Virginia C. Gordon of the Preventative Diagnostic Corporation in Santa Monica, California, along with a

---

[16] "Newsletter," Mobilization For Animals, ([Columbus, Ohio]: MFA, 1987).

[17] Martin L. Stephens, Ph.D. Alternatives to Current Uses in Research, Safety Testing, and Education. (Washington, D.C.: The Humane Society of the United States, 1986) 35.

43

team of fellow researchers, set out to develop a test that could measure the potential for eye irritation and possibly qualify as a replacement for the Draize Eye Irritancy Test.[18]

The test, called the Eytex Screen, can determine the irritation potential of substances used in cosmetics and household products. The test uses a synthetic matrix of protein that behaves in the same manner as the protein found in an animal's eye. When the synthetic protein is exposed to ocular irritants, the subsequent reaction provides the same information as the Draize Eye Test.[19] This test is now being used by some industrial and academic laboratories.

CAM Test (Chorioallantoic Membrane Assay)

A test using the chorioallantoic membrane of the chicken egg was developed by Dr. Joseph Leighton and Dr. Ruy Tchao of the Medical College of Pennsylvania, in 1985, to test the effects of toxic compounds and substances.

The egg membrane test is one of the most promising and humane alternatives to the Draize Eye Test. The membrane contains blood vessels very similar to those found in the human eye.

The test is performed by removing a tiny section of the shell of a fertilized egg. The inner membrane is carefully exposed, and a small amount of test substance is applied. The membrane is sensitive, but as it has no nerve cells, no pain is involved.

Reactions such as inflammation and irritation of the blood vessels are clearly observed, and recorded.

Computer Simulation and Mathematical Models

Data collected from past experiments and research originally done on live laboratory animals can be used to create

---

[18.] Dr. Christopher P. Kelly, "Eytex: an In-Vitro Method Of Predicting Ocular Safety," D. & CI. August 1988: 34.

[19.] Ibid: 38.

computer simulation of the reaction of tissue cells and organs to chemical substances.

Computer simulation of experiments could eliminate the use of animal experiments not only in research laboratories, but in classrooms as well.

Data revealing toxic reactions can be stored on computer and made available to companies and laboratories wishing to determine the toxicity of certain products, without repeating animal tests.

Mathematical models are now used in diagnosis and data processing, and can be used to predict the effect of a toxic substance on the human system. Models can also be used to predict the amount of a new, untested substance required to kill 50 percent of a group of test animals. Using mathematical structures, computers can compare the toxicity of the new substance to the toxicity of similar tested toxins and predict the lethal dose of the new substance.

Human Clinical Studies

The testing of new cosmetics made from ingredients established as non-toxic can be done safely on humans. Human volunteers are used in clinical case studies by cruelty-free cosmetic companies that not only want to avoid animal experiments, but also want to offer the consumer products containing ingredients established as non-harmful.

The testing of products on humans produces more valuable results than animal tests because volunteers can provide a verbal as well as a visible reaction to the products.

Bacteria Cultures and Protozoan Studies

As the single cell of many species of bacteria and protozoa react to toxins and irritants in a way similar to the cells of human beings, this kind of test offers a viable alternative to animal tests. In addition, bacteria and protozoa reproduce extremely rapidly and are easily monitored, controlled, and stored, at a very low cost.

The cell of both bacteria and protozoa can be monitored for genetic changes, mutation, and chromosome damage, a distinct advantage over traditional tests, as the reaction of cells to chemicals can not be readily monitored in live animals.

Bacteria and protozoa are presently being used to study cancer, birth defects, and environmental problems. They can also be used to test new chemicals that constitute cosmetics and household products.

Placenta
Since it is discarded after childbirth, the placenta is the most available and least costly human organ. The use of the placenta not only eliminates ethical concern, but also provides a unique source of human material without posing danger to the patient.

The human placenta is highly sensitive and responsive to chemicals. Degrees of membrane damage and cell death can be monitored and recorded to provide a guideline of human tissue reactions to the toxins. Test results would relate directly to human beings.

Chapter 4

STOP ANIMAL TESTING: WHAT YOU CAN DO

…we must learn to flex our consumer muscle for animal rights. The market gets what the market demands, and our demands for an end to animal testing must be heard loud and clear.

PEOPLE FOR THE ETHICAL TREATMENT
OF ANIMALS, NEWSLETTER, 1987

PURCHASE CRUELTY-FREE PRODUCTS

Stop animal testing of cosmetics and household products by becoming a concerned individual and caring consumer. Use the list in this book to acquaint yourself with cruelty-free products and buy only those products that you know are *not* tested on animals. Many are available at health or natural food stores, or in drug and department stores.

You have a choice. Once you know the facts behind the testing of cosmetics and household products, you can act on your beliefs, by choosing which products you wish to purchase: products that have been tested on animals or products that have not.

As an individual consumer, you cannot stop animal testing, but together we have the power to persuade and reform, simply by exercising our choice of purchase.[20]

WRITE LETTERS TO THE COMPANIES

Write to the cosmetic companies listed in Chapter 2, and tell them that you are aware that they are conducting animal testing of their products. Ask for a confirmation. Ask specifically if they do test their products, including raw materials, on laboratory animals. Demand, as a concerned customer, that they sponsor and adopt alternatives to test their products.

Receiving letters in protest of animal testing of cosmetics makes the cosmetic industry realize that this practice is no longer acceptable.

Most companies that you contact will no doubt write back stating that the reason they conduct animal tests is for the sake of "human safety". They will tell you that by conducting tests on animals, their products are established as "safe", as they conduct all animal tests "...for the protection of human subjects."[21] They will tell you that by conducting tests on animals, their products can be used without harmful side affects.

The excuses will by many, and the letters will be cleverly worded to give deceiving impressions. However, unless the reply clearly states that they do not conduct any animal tests, of *any kind, on their products, or employ an outside laboratory to test their products or raw materials,* you can be certain that some form of animal testing is being carried out.[22]

Learn to read between the lines. The replies usually give

---

[20] "Issues: Animal Testing and Cosmetics," The Body Shop International, ([Don Mills, Ontario]: [The Body Shop International] n.d.) 1–3.

[21] Noxema Inc., letter to Ms. Tita Zierer, December 22, 1986.

[22] News Abstracts," *AFAAR*, Winter 1988/1989: 1.

the impression that the companies that do test on animals are doing their best to advocate and promote alternatives, for example a reply such as the following: "As a member of the CFTA, [our company] supports and participates in this trade association's ongoing program to develop alternatives...." However, while the support of alternatives is mentioned, it is not clear that they are funding or directing financial assistance energetically enough to produce results.[23]

Unfortunately, their reassurance of financial support has been repeated to the public since 1981, and after eight years and their alleged spending of millions, they have not come up with a single validated replacement. Moreover, they continue to blame the government for their failure. Cosmetic companies are, after all, well experienced in cover-ups!

The following paragraphs are taken from a letter received from The American Fund For Alternatives to Animal Research:

> Several newly developed alternatives to the Draize Test, which have done well in beginning comparison tests, are ready for further validation studies. Yet, over a year has elapsed, and there has been no move on the part of the [cosmetic] industry [including the sponsors of the comparisons] either to publish the results of these first comparison studies, or to continue the validation process.
>
> The results of the comparison tests [with Draize Tests] done at Colgate Palmolive in 1985 on the CAM Alternative Test developed by Joseph Leighton, M.D., and Dr. Ruy Tchao, are not available to the public.[24]

[23.] Ibid: 3.

[24.] Dr. Ethel Thurston, letter to The Soap and Detergent Association, as cited in ibid, Summer 1987.

> We, [The American Fund for Alternatives to Animal Research] have tried on several occasions to obtain the figures of other 1985 comparison studies, done by The Soap and Detergent Association of New York (SDA), on the CAM, and some other Draize replacement tests, but without success. [25]

It almost seems that validation of the tests to replace the Draize are being purposely delayed, and the results are being suppressed!

Public pressure is needed to force these companies to carry on with the validation process and to publish the results. Write to Colgate-Palmolive, Chairman, 300 Park Avenue, New York, New York, 10022, and to The Soap and Detergent Association, 475 Park Avenue, New York, New York, 10016, and to the Canadian Cosmetic, Toiletry and Fragrance Association, 24 Merton Street, Toronto, Ontario, Canada, M4A 1A1. Advise them that as a concerned consumer, you are well aware of the lack of published comparison studies and of the halt to continue further research and testing of the validation process. Tell them that you want to know how the results of the alternatives compare to the Draize Test, that you want to see the results published, and that, if the validation is not yet completed, you want to know when it will be completed. Express your concern about the length of the time that is being wasted waiting for validation and about the animals that are suffering unnecessarily during this time.

By the same token, write to companies that do *not* test on animals, and whose products you have tried and are satisfied with, and thank them for their compassion and concern for our fellow creatures. Let them know that you purchase their products. Suggest ways that their products can be

---

[25.] Ibid, Fall 1987: 1.

improved as well as retailers they can contact in your area for wider distribution.

JOIN ANIMAL WELFARE ORGANIZATIONS

Join as many organizations as possible that are dedicated to animal welfare. Write to them for membership and for literature on current animal issues. Use the information you receive to inform local media personnel, friends, and neighbours.

When contacting the media, urge them to report and discuss animal exploitation by manufacturers of cosmetics and personal care products.

Write letters to the editor of local newspapers and magazines, explaining in detail the meaning and availability of "cruelty-free" products and "alternatives" to the use of laboratory animals.

DISCUSS THE ISSUE

Most people will not knowingly support cruelty done to animals, but many are not aware that such barbaric practices are taking place, much less taking place legally.

Organize forums to discuss the issue of animal testing to be held at women's groups, church groups, youth organizations, service and volunteer groups, and other institutions that may be responsive. Discuss the issue with friends. Be positive and unemotional.

Alert your family and co-workers to the abuse of animals in cosmetic and product testing. Encourage them to purchase cruelty-free products whenever they can. As concerned individuals, we must inform others so that they will also demand non-violent methods of product testing from the cosmetic industry.[26]

[26.] "Facts on Cosmetic and Product Testing in North America," The Toronto Humane Society, ([Toronto]: [THS], n.d.).

VOTE FOR CRUELTY-FREE

Promote legislation to protect animals. Write to Congress Representatives and local Members of Parliament, suggesting that they introduce a bill that will prohibit eye irritancy and toxicity animal tests for cosmetics, personal care, and household products. Such a bill would also encourage manufacturers to develop new products from ingredients established as safe and non-toxic.

Request that adequate attention and response be given to your inquiries and concerns. Demand, as a citizen, that your elected member of government support a ban of the use of animals for cosmetic and product testing.

Chapter 5

CRUELTY-FREE COMPANIES IN CANADA AND THE UNITED STATES

If we truly were concerned about product safety, we would require companies to rely on ingredients which are already known to be safe in the development of new consumer products.

AURORA ALBERTI, M.D., BETHESDA, MARYLAND

You can have a business that's socially responsible as well as successful. It's really unnecessary to keep testing and retesting.

KATE CHAPPELL, TOM'S OF MAINE

The companies listed below test their products on human volunteers, *not* animals. Since these companies use only natural ingredients that have been used safely for hundreds of years, they can be tested without the danger of harmful reactions.

By choosing products from the manufacturers listed here, you are applying the consumer pressure that will help eliminate animal testing of cosmetics and household products.

This list has been compiled from information received from the manufacturers, and is offered in good faith.

ABRACADABRA INC.
PO Box 1040
Guerneville, California
95446
Personal Care: bath products, cosmetic clays; **Catalogue; Shop by Mail**

ADITI-NUTRI-SENTIALS
779 Broadway
New York, New York
10013
Cosmetics; Personal Care: hair care products; **Catalogue; Shop by Mail**

AFFIRMATIVE ALTERNATIVES
PO Box 33492
Granada Hills, California
91344
Cosmetics: colour make-up; **Personal Care:** skin and hair care products **Household Products; Catalogue; Shop by Mail**

AFRICAN BIO-BOTANICA
7509 North West 13th Boulevard
Gainesville, Florida
32606
Personal Care: bath and hair care products; **Catalogue; Shop by Mail**

ALBA BOTANICA COSMETICS
PO Box 1858
Santa Monica, California
90406
Personal Care: bath care products, men's toiletries; **Catalogue; Shop by Mail**

ALEXANDRA AVERY (PURELY NATURAL)
Northrup Creek
Clatskanie, Oregon
97016
Personal Care: skin and bath care products, perfumes; **Catalogue; Shop by Mail**

ALFIN FRAGRANCES, INC.
15 Maple Street
Norwood, New Jersey
17648
Personal Care: bath products, perfumes

ALIDA
PO Box 9517
Fort Collins, Colorado
80525
Household Products; Catalogue

54

ALLEN'S NATURALLY
PO Box 514
Farmington, Michigan
48332
Household Products; Catalogue; Shop by Mail

ALVA-AMCO PHARMACAL COSMETICS
6625 Avondale Avenue
Chicago, Illinois
60631
Cosmetics; Personal Care

AMBERWOOD
Route 1, Box 206
Milner, Georgia
30257
Cosmetics: colour make-up; Personal Care: skin, bath, and hair care products, men's toiletries; Household Products; Catalogue; Shop by Mail

AMERICAN COSMETIC MANUFACTURING LABS
599 - 4th Street
San Francisco, California
94107
Cosmetics; Personal Care

AMERICAN MERFLUAN INC.
41 Sutter Street, Suite 1153
San Francisco, California
94104
Personal Care; Catalogue; Shop by Mail

ANANDA COUNTRY PRODUCTS
14618 Tyler Fort Road
Nevada City, California
95959
Personal Care: perfumes; Catalogue; Shop by Mail

ANDALINA
Tory Hill
Warner, New Hampshire
03278
Personal Care: bath products; Catalogue; Shop by Mail

ANIMAL LOVE
337 North Buena Vista
Burbank, California
91505
Personal Care: skin and bath care products

AROMA VERA CO.
PO Box 3609
Culver City, California
90231
Personal Care: bath products; Catalogue; Shop by Mail

ATTA LAVI
1105 Massachusetts Avenue, 6A
Cambridge, Massachusetts
02138
Personal Care

AUBREY ORGANICS
4419 North Manhattan Avenue
Tampa, Florida
33614
Cosmetics: colour make-up; Personal Care: skin and hair care products; Catalogue; Shop by Mail

AURA CACIA INC.
PO Box 391
Weaverville, California
96093

Personal Care: skin and bath care products, perfumes; **Catalogue; Shop by Mail**

AUROMERE: AYURVEDIC IMPORTS
1291 Weber Street
Pomona, California
91768

Personal Care: skin and bath care products, perfumes; **Catalogue; Shop by Mail**

AURORA HENNA
120 - 3rd Avenue North
Minneapolis, Minnesota
55401

Personal Care: skin and hair care products

AUTUMN HARP
28 Rockydale Road
Bristol, Vermont
05443

Personal Care: skin and baby care products; **Catalogue; Shop by Mail**

AVEDA CORPORATION
321 Lincoln Street North East
Minneapolis, Minnesota
55413

Cosmetics: colour make-up **Personal Care:** hair care products (both retailed at beauty salons and beauty schools in North America under the brand name "Indra")

BABY TOUCH LTD.
100 Sandpiper Circle
Corte Madera, California
94925

Personal Care; Catalogue; Shop by Mail

BARE ESCENTUALS
809 University Avenue
Los Gatos, California
95030

Cosmetics: colour make-up; **Personal Care:** perfumes; **Catalogue; Shop by Mail**

BAUBIOLOGIE HARDWARE
PO Box 51250, Suite 125-A
Pacific Grove, California
93950

Household Products; Catalogue; Shop by Mail

BAUDELAIRE INC.
Forest Road
Marlow, New Hampshire
03456

Personal Care; skin, hair, and bath care products; **Catalogue; Shop by Mail**

BEAUTY NATURALLY
PO Box 429, 57 Bosque Road
Fairfax, California
94930

Cosmetics: colour make-up; **Personal Care:** skin and hair care products; **Catalogue; Shop by Mail**

BEAUTY WITHOUT CRUELTY LTD.
451 Queen Anne Road
Teaneck, New Jersey
07666
Cosmetics: colour make-up; **Personal Care:** skin, hair, and bath care products, perfumes; **Catalogue; Shop by Mail**

BELVEDERE LABS
20688 Corsair Boulevard
Hayward, California
94544
Personal Care: skin and hair care products

BEVAN
PO Box 20072, Dag Hammarskjold Ctr.
New York, New York
10017-7820
Personal Care: skin care products; **Catalogue; Shop by Mail**

BIOKOSMA
841 South Main Street
Spring Valley, New York
10977
Head Office:
CH-9642 Ebnat-Kappel
Switzerland
Personal Care: bath and hair care products; **Catalogue; Shop by Mail**

BIO LINE INC.
8337 Pennsylvania Avenue South, Suite 26
Minneapolis, Minnesota
55431-1738
Personal Care: skin and hair care products; **Household Products; Catalogue; Shop by Mail**

BODY LOVE NATURAL COSMETICS
PO Box 7542
Santa Cruz, California
96061
Personal Care: skin care products; **Catalogue; Shop by Mail**

THE BODY SHOP INTERNATIONAL
45 Horse Hill Road
Hanover Texaco Center
Cedar Knolls, New Jersey
07927-2003
15 Prince Andrew Place
Don Mills, Ontario
M3C 2H2
Cosmetics: colour make-up; **Personal Care:** skin, hair, and bath care products, perfumes, men's toiletries; **Catalogue; Shop by Mail**

THE BODY SHOP USA
(not affiliated with The Body Shop International)
1431 - 7th Street
Berkeley, California
94710
Personal Care: skin and bath care products, perfumes; **Catalogue; Shop by Mail**

BOERLIND, ANNEMARIE (OF GERMANY)
PO Box 1487
New London, New Hampshire
03257

210-A Denison Street
Markham, Ontario
L3R 1B6

Head Office: 7260 Calw-Altburg
Schwartzwald, West Germany

Personal Care: skin and bath care products; **Catalogue; Shop by Mail**

BONNE SANTE HEALTH PRODUCTS
462 62nd Street
Brooklyn, New York
11220

Personal Care; Catalogue; Shop by Mail

SHIRLEY BROWN
17636 Corte Potosi
San Diego, California
92128

Cosmetics: colour make-up; **Personal Care:** skin and hair care products; **Household Products; Catalogue; Shop by Mail**

CAMILLA HEPPER
(c/o Baraka Company)
4338 Center Gate
San Antonio, Texas
78217

Personal Care: skin and bath care products; **Catalogue; Shop by Mail**

CARBONA PRODUCTS
330 Calyer Street
Brooklyn, New York
11222

Household Products; Catalogue; Shop by Mail

CARME
84 Galli Drive
Novato, California
94947

Personal Care: skin and baby care products; **Catalogue; Shop by Mail** (Carmé products include Country Roads, Jojoba Farms, Loanda, Sleepy Hollow Botanical, Mill Creek, and Mountain Herbery.)

CAROLE'S COSMETICS
3081 Klondike Avenue
Costa Mesa, California
92626

Cosmetics: colour make-up; **Personal Care:** skin and hair care products; **Catalogue; Shop by Mail**

CATE VENTURES
38 Kalahkaua Avenue
Hilo, Hawaii
96720

Personal Care

CERTAN-DRI (division of Leon Products Inc.)
PO Box 24845
Jackonsville, Florida
32241

Personal Care; Catalogue; Shop by Mail

CHENTI PRODUCTS INC.
21093 Forbes Avenue
Hayward, California
94545

Personal Care: skin and hair care products; **Catalogue; Shop by Mail**

CHICO-SAN COSMETICS AND TOILETRIES
1264 Humboldt Avenue
PO Box 1004
Chico, California
95927

Personal Care

A CLEAR ALTERNATIVE
8707 West Lane
Magnolia, Texas
77355

Personal Care

CLEARLY NATURAL PRODUCTS
PO Box 750024
Petaluma, California
94975-0024

Personal Care: bath care products; **Catalogue; Shop by Mail**

CLIENTELE
5207 North West 163rd Street
Miami, Florida
33014

Cosmetics: colour make-up; **Personal Care:** skin care products; **Catalogue; Shop by Mail** (Clientele products are sold at Neiman-Marcus in Chicago, and through the Neimen-Marcus catalogue.)

COLOUR QUEST
210 South 5th Street
St. Charles, Illinois
60174

Cosmetics: colour make-up; **Personal Care:** skin and nail care products; **Catalogue; Shop by Mail**

COLUMBIA MAINCURE MFG. CO.
1 Seneca Place
Greenwich, Conneticut
06830

Personal Care: nail care products

COME TO YOUR SENSES
321 Cedar Avenue South
Minneapolis, Minnesota
55454

Personal Care: skin care products;

COMFORT MANUFACTURING CO.
1056 West Van Buren Street
Chicago, Illinois
60607

Personal Care: skin care products, men's toiletries

COMMUNITY SOAP FACTORY
PO Box 32057
Washington, District of Columbia
20007

Personal Care: skin and hair care products; **Catalogue; Shop by Mail**

COMPASSIONATE
CONSUMER, THE
PO Box 27
Jericho, New York
11753
Cosmetics: colour make-up; **Personal Care:** skin, hair, and bath care products; **Household Products; Catalogue; Shop by Mail**

COMPASSIONATE
COSMETICS
PO Box 3534
Glendale, California
91201
Cosmetics: colour make-up; **Personal Care**

COMPASSIONATE
PRODUCTS
718 Crane Street
Catasanqua, Pennsylvania
18032
Cosmetics: colour make-up; **Household Products; Catalogue; Shop by Mail**

COOL PRODUCTS
1168-B Massachusetts Avenue
Cambridge, Massachusetts
02138
Personal Care: skin and body care products; **Catalogue; Shop by Mail**

COUNTRY COMFORT
28537 Nuevo Valley Drive, Box 3
Nueva, California
92367
Personal Care: skin and baby care products; **Catalogue; Shop by Mail**

COUNTRY ROADS
84 Galli Drive
Novato, California
94949
Personal Care: skin and hair care products; **Catalogue; Shop by Mail**

CREATURE CARE
PO Box 763, 9009 South Street
Monte Rio, California
95462
Cosmetics: colour make-up; **Personal Care:** skin, hair, and bath care products; **Catalogue; Shop by Mail**

CRUELTY-FREE COSMETICS
PLUS
38 East 89th Street
New York, New York
10128
Cosmetics: colour make-up; **Personal Care:** skin care products

DESERT ESSENCE
COSMETICS
PO Box 588
Topanga, California
90290
Personal Care: skin and hair care products; **Catalogue; Shop by Mail**

DODGE CHEMICALS CO. INC.
165 Rindge Ext.
Cambridge, Massachusetts
02140
Household Products

DR. E. H. BRONNER
PO Box 28
Escondido, Califonia
92025
Personal Care

DR. HAUSCHKA COSMETICS INC.
Meadowbrook West
Wyoming, Rhode Island
02898
Cosmetics: colour make-up; **Personal Care**

EARTH CARE
714 - 24th Avenue East
Seattle, Washington
98112
Personal Care

EARTH SCIENCE, INC.
PO Box 1925
Corona, California
91720
Personal Care: skin, hair and bath care products, men's toiletries; **Catalogue; Shop by Mail**

ECCO BELLA
125 Pompton Plains Crossroads
Wayne, New Jersey
07470
Cosmetics: colour make-up; **Personal Care:** skin, hair, and bath care products, perfumes, men's toiletries; **Household Products; Catalogue; Shop by Mail**

ESPREE
PO Box 160249
Irving, Texas
75016
Personal Care: skin and hair care products, men's toiletries

ESPRESS OF SAGINAW
300 St. Andrews Road
Saginaw, Michigan
48603
Personal Care: skin care products

ESSENTIALS
Rd. 2, Box 160-A
Ghent, New York
12075
Personal Care: perfumes; **Catalogue; Shop by Mail**

EVE COSMETICS
PO Box 131
Pebble Beach, California
93953
Personal Care: hair care products

FASHION TWO TWENTY
1263 South Chillicothe Road, Box 220
Aurora, Ohio
44202

1340 Main Street East
Hamilton, Ontario L8K 1B5
Cosmetics: colour make-up; **Personal Care:** skin, bath, and nail care products, perfumes, men's toiletries; **Catalogue; Shop by Mail**

FAULTLESS STARCH/ BON AMI CO.
1025 West 8th Street
Kansas City, Missouri
64100
Household Products

FINELLE COSMETICS
137 Marston Street
Lawrence, Maryland
01842
Cosmetics: colour make-up; **Personal Care:** skin and bath care products; **Catalogue; Shop by Mail**

4-D HOBE MARKETING
201 South McKemy Street
Chandley, Arizona
85226
Personal Care: skin and hair care products;**Catalogue; Shop by Mail**

FRONTIER HERBS
Box 299
Norway, Iowa
52318
Personal Care

A. J. FUNK & CO.
1471 Timber Drive
Elgin, Illinois
60120
Household Products; Catalogue; Shop by Mail

GENERAL NUTRITION
PO Box 349
1301 - 39th Street
Fargo, North Dakota
58107
Personal Care: skin and hair care products; **Catalogue; Shop by Mail**

GERMINATION/BUSHWACKY
PO Box 279, Station "V"
Toronto, Ontario
M6R 3A5
Personal Care: skin and hair care products; **Catalogue; Shop by Mail**

GIOVANNI COSMETICS INC.
PO Box 205
Reseda, California
91335
Personal Care: hair care products; **Catalogue; Shop by Mail**

GOING FIRST CLASS
PO Box 266
Pocono Manor, Pennsylvania
18349-1266
Personal Care: skin and hair care products; **Household Products; Catalogue; Shop by Mail**

GOLDEN LOTUS
PO Box 1323
Englewood, Colourado
80150
Personal Care: skin and hair care products; **Household Products; Catalogue; Shop by Mail**

GOLDWELL COSMETICS
9015 Junction Drive
Annopolis Junction, Maryland
20701
Personal Care: hair care products; **Catalogue; Shop by Mail** (Goldwell products are used in many beauty salons in North America and Europe)

GRANNY'S OLD FASHIONED PRODUCTS
3581 East Milton Street
Pasadena, California
91107
Personal Care: hair care products; **Household Products; Catalogue; Shop by Mail**

GRUENE KOSMETIK
256 South Robertson Boulevard
Beverley Hills, California
90211
Personal Care: skin and hair care products; **Catalogue; Shop by Mail**

HAIN PURE FOOD COMPANY
13660 South Figuera
Los Angeles, California
90061
Personal Care: skin and bath care products; **Catalogue; Shop by Mail**

HAWAIIAN RESOURCES
1123 Kapahulu Avenue
Honolulu, Hawaii
96816
Personal Care: skin care products for tanning; **Catalogue; Shop by Mail**

HEART'S DESIRE
1478 University Avenue
Number 261
Berkeley, California
94702
Cosmetics: colour make-up; **Personal Care:** skin, hair, and bath care products; **Household Products; Catalogue; Shop by Mail**

HEAVENLY SOAP
5948 East 30th Street
Tucson, Arizona
85711
Personal Care: skin and bath care products; **Catalogue; Shop by Mail**

HOME SERVICE PRODUCTS CO.
230 Willow Street
Bound Brook, New Jersey
08805
Household Products

HUISH CHEMICAL CO.
3540-W 1987 South
Salt Lake City, Utah
84125
Household Products; Catalogue; Shop by Mail

HUMANE ALTERNATIVE PRODUCTS
8 Hutchins Street
Concord, New Hampshire
03301
Cosmetics: colour make-up; **Household Products; Catalogue; Shop by Mail**

HUMPHREY'S PHARMACAL, INC.
63 Meadow Road
Rutherford, New Jersey
07070
Personal Care

I CARE COSMETICS AND CLEANSERS
1216 North Brighton
Burbank, California
91505
Cosmetics; Household Products; Catalogue; Shop by Mail

IDA GRAE NATURE'S COLOURS COSMETICS
424 Laverne Avenue
Mill Valley, California
94941
Cosmetics: colour make-up; Personal Care: skin care products; Catalogue; Shop by Mail

IMAGE LABORATORIES
PO Box 55016, Metro Station
Los Angeles, California
90055
Personal Care: hair care products

INFINITY HERBAL PRODUCTS
333 Rimrock Road
Toronto, Ontario
M3J 3C6
Personal Care: hair care products; Household Products; Catalogue; Shop by Mail

INSTITUTE OF TRICHOLOGY (Tri Products)
1619 Reed Street
Lakewood, California
80215
Personal Care: hair care products; Catalogue; Shop by Mail

INTERNATIONAL ROTEX INC.
PO Box 20697
Reno, Nevada
89515
Household Products

INTERNATURAL
PO Box 580, Shaker Street
South Sutton, New Hampshire
03273
Cosmetics: colour make-up; Personal Care: skin, hair, and bath care products, men's toiletries; Catalogue; Shop by Mail

IRMA SHORELL INC.
720 5th Avenue
New York, New York
10019
Personal Care: skin, hair, and bath care products; Catalogue; Shop by Mail

IT'S NATURAL, INC.
733 Filbert Street, 2nd Floor
Pittsburg, Pennsylvania
15232
Personal Care

JACKI'S MAGIC LOTION
158 A Street, Number 7A
Ashland, Oregon
97520

Personal Care: skin care products; **Catalogue; Shop by Mail**

JAMIESON'S
1 St. Clair Avenue East, Suite 802
Toronto, Ontario
M4T 2V7

Personal Care: skin care products

JASON NATURAL PRODUCTS
8468 Warner Drive
Culver City, California
90232

Personal Care; Catalogue; Shop by Mail

JEANNE ROSE HERBAL BODY WORKS
219-A Carl Street
San Francisco, California
94117

Personal Care: skin, hair, and bath care products; **Catalogue; Shop by Mail**

JOHN PAUL MITCHELL SYSTEM
26455 Golden Valley Road
Santa Clara Valley, California
91350

Personal Care: hair care products; **Catalogue; Shop by Mail** (John Paul Mitchell products are used in many beauty salons in Canada and the U.S.)

JOJOBA FARMS
84 Galli Drive
Novata, California
94947

Personal Care: hair care products; **Catalogue; Shop by Mail**

JOJOBA RESOURCES
10201 North 21st Street, #10
Phoenix, Arizona
85021

Personal Care: Skin, hair and nail care products

JURLIQUE COSMETICS
16 Starlit Drive
Northport, New York
11768

Personal Care: skin and hair care products; **Household Products; Catalogue; Shop by Mail**

KEY WEST FRAGRANCE AND COSMETIC FACTORY
Box 771
524 Front Street
Key West, Florida
33041

Cosmetics: colour make-up; **Personal Care:** skin care products, fragrances

KIMBERLY SAYER INC.
61 West 82nd Street
Number 5A
New York, New York
10024

Personal Care: skin and bath care products; **Catalogue: Shop by Mail**

KIM'S KRUELTY-FREE PRODUCTS
4 Wooden Court Way
Baltimore, Maryland
21208
Cosmetics: colour make-up;
Personal Care: skin, hair and bath care products, fragrances, men's toiletries; **Household Products; Catalogue; Shop by Mail**

KISS MY FACE
PO Box 804
New Paltz, New York
12561
Personal Care: skin, hair and bath care products; **Catalogue; Shop by Mail**

KMS
6807 Highway 299 East
Bella Vista, California
96008
(Products are used in many beauty salons throughout North America)
Personal Care: hair care products

KSA JOJOBA
19025 Parthenia Street
Number 200
Northridge, California
91324
Personal Care: skin, hair and bath care products, perfumes

LA COUPE HAIR PRODUCTS
694 Madison Avenue
New York, New York
10021

1115 Sherbrooke Street West
Montreal, Quebec
H3A 1H3
Cosmetics: colour make-up; **Personal Care:** hair care products

LANZA RESEARCH LABORATORIES
1440 East Arrow Highway
Number 7
Irwindale, California
91706
Personal Care: hair care products; **Catalogue; Shop by Mail**

LEICHNER'S STAGE MAKE-UP
(c/o Costume House)
284 King Street West
Toronto, Ontario
M5V 1J2
Cosmetics: colour theatrical make-up; **Catalogue; Shop by Mail**

LEVLAND/NATURE'S GATE
9183-5 Kelvin Street
Chatsworth, California
91311
Personal Care: skin, hair and bath care products; **Catalogue; Shop by Mail**

LIFE TREE PRODUCTS
PO Box 513
Grafton, California
95444
Personal Care: bath care products, men's toiletries; **Household Products; Catalogue; Shop by Mail**

LILY OF THE DESERT
2001 Walnut Hill Lane
Irving, Texas
75038
Personal Care: skin care products; **Catalogue; Shop by Mail**

LIVOS PLANT CHEMISTRY
614 Agua Fria Street
Santa Fe, New Mexico
87501
Household Products; Catalogue; Shop by Mail

LOANDA HERBAL PRODUCTS
84 Galli Drive
Novato, California
94947
Personal Care: bath care products; **Catalogue; Shop by Mail**

M. & N. PRODUCTS
PO Box 4502
Anaheim, California
92803
Personal Care

MAGIC AMERICAN CHEMICAL CORPORATION
23700 Mercantile Road
Cleveland, Ohio
44122
209 Brunel Road
Mississauga, Ontario
L4Z 1X3
Household Products

THE MAGIC OF ALOE, INC.
7300 North Crescent Boulevard
Pennsauken, New Jersey
08110
Cosmetics: colour make-up; **Personal Care:** skin and hair care products, men's toiletries; **Catalogue; Shop by Mail**

MAKAMINA INC.
PO Box 307
Wallingford, Pennsylvania
19056
Personal Care: skin and hair care products; **Catalogue; Shop by Mail**

MARKS AND SPENCER
3770 Nashua Drive
Mississauga, Ontario
L4V 1M6
(Marks and Spencer outlets are located throughout Canada)
Cosmetics: colour make-up; **Personal Care:** skin, hair and bath care products, men's toiletries; **Catalogue**

MARLY SAVON CLAIR
PO Box 54841
Terminal Annex
Los Angeles, California
90054
Personal Care

MARTIN VON MYERING
422 Jay Street
Pittsburgh, Pennsylvania
15212
Personal Care; Catalogue; Shop by Mail

MAVALA NAIL CARE PRODUCTS
CH-1205
Geneva
Switzerland
(Mavala products are widely sold in North America)
Personal Care: nail care products

MIA ROSE PRODUCTS INC.
1374 Logan Avenue
Unit C
Costa Mesa, California
92626
Personal Care; Catalogue; Shop by Mail

MICHAEL'S
4200 North 22nd Street
McAllen, Texas
78504
Personal Care: skin care products; **Catalogue; Shop by Mail**

MICROBALANCED PRODUCTS
25 Alladin Avenue
Dumont, New Jersey
07628
Personal Care: skin and bath care products; **Catalogue; Shop by Mail**

MILD AND NATURAL
84 Galli Drive
Novato, California
94947
Personal Care: skin care products; **Catalogue; Shop by Mail**

MILL CREEK
84 Galli Drive
Novato, California
94947
Personal Care: skin, hair and bath care products; **Catalogue; Shop by Mail**

MIRA LINDER HEALTH SPAS
29935 Northwestern Highway
Southfield, Michigan
48034

108 Avenue Road
Toronto, Ontario
M5R 2H3
Cosmetics: colour make-up; **Personal Care:** skin, hair and bath care products

MISS C'S CLOSET
524-A Bloomfield Avenue
Verona, New Jersey
07044
Cosmetics: colour make-up; **Personal Care:** skin, hair and bath care products; **Household Products; Catalogue; Shop by Mail**

MOUNTAIN HERBERY
84 Galli Drive
Novato, California
94947

Personal Care: skin and hair care products; **Catalogue; Shop by Mail**

MOUNTAIN OCEAN COSMETICS AND TOILETRIES
4830 Pearl Street
Boulder, Colorado
80301

Personal Care: skin care products; **Catalogue; Shop by Mail**

MULGUM HOLLOW FARMS
PO Box 745
Longview, Washington
98632

Household Products; Catalogue; Shop by Mail

THE MURPHY-PHOENIX COMPANY
Corporate Place, Suite 200
25800 Science Park Drive
Beachwood, Ohio
44122

Household Products; Catalogue; Shop by Mail

MY BROTHER'S KEEPER
PO Box 1769
Richmond, Indiana
47375

Cosmetics: colour make-up; **Personal Care:** skin, hair and bath care products, perfumes, men's toiletries; **Household Products; Catalogue; Shop by Mail**

NATURADE COSMETICS
7100 East Jackson Street
Paramount, California
90723

Cosmetics: colour make-up; **Personal Care:** skin and hair care products; **Catalogue; Shop by Mail**

NATURAL ANIMAL (ECO-SAFE LABORATORIES, INC.)
PO Box 8702
Oakland, California
94662

Pet Care Products; Catalogue; Shop by Mail

NATURAL COSMETICS
306 East 2nd Street
Morris, Minneapolis
56267

Personal Care; Catalogue

NATURAL ORGANICS COSMETICS
10 Daniel Street
Farmingdale, New York
11735

Personal Care; Catalogue

NATURALL BRAND PRODUCTS
PO Box 28
Walled Lake, Michigan
48088

Household Products; Catalogue; Shop by Mail

69

NATURE BASICS
61 Main Street
Lancaster, New Hampshire
03584
Cosmetics: colour make-up; Personal Care: skin care products; Household Products; Catalogue; Shop by Mail

NATURE COSMETICS
881 Alma Real
Suite 101
Pacific Palisades, California
90272
Cosmetics: colour make-up; Personal Care: skin and nail care products

NATURE DE FRANCE
444 Park Avenue South
New York, New York
10016
Personal Care: skin and hair care products; Catalogue; Shop by Mail

NATURE'S COLORS
424 Laverne Avenue
Mill Valley, California
94941
Cosmetics: colour make-up; Personal Care

NATURE'S GATE HERBAL COSMETICS
9183-5 Kelvin Street
Chatsworth, California
91311
Cosmetics: colour make-up; Catalogue

NATURE'S PLUS
10 Daniel Street
Farmingdale, New York
11735
Personal Care: skin and hair care products; Catalogue; Shop by Mail

NATUROPATHIC LABORATORIES
PO Box 11241
St. Petersburgh, Florida
33733
Personal Care; Catalogue; Shop by Mail

NEW AGE PRODUCTS
16100 North Highway 101
Willits, California
95490
Household Products; Catalogue; Shop by Mail

NEW WORLD MINERALS
4459 East Rochelle Avenue
Las Vegas, Nevada
89121-6430
Personal Care: bath care products; Catalogue; Shop by Mail

NEWAY
150 Causeway Street
Boston, Massachusetts
02114
Household Products; Catalogue; Shop by Mail

NEXXUS
PO Box 4730
Santa Barbara, California
93103
Personal Care: hair care products

NO COMMON SCENTS
King's Yard
Yellow Springs, Ohio
45387
Personal Care: skin care products, perfumes; **Household Products; Catalogue; Shop by Mail**

NORTH COUNTRY SOAP
7888 Country road
Number 6
Maple Plain, Minnesota
55359
Personal Care: bath care products; **Catalogue ; Shop by Mail**

NU SKIN INTERNATIONAL INC.
750 North 200 West Street
Number 104
Provo, Utah
84601
Personal Care: skin care products; **Catalogue; Shop by Mail**

NUTRI-METICS INTERNATIONAL
19501 East Walnut Drive
Box 1286
City of Industry, California
91748
3915 - 61st Avenue South East
Calgary, Alberta
T2C 1V5
Cosmetics: colour make-up; **Personal Care:** skin, bath and nail care products, men's toiletries; **Household Products; Catalogue; Shop by Mail**

OMBRA
(c/o Raha Enterprises Limited)
1589 The Queensway
Units 10 & 11
Toronto, Ontario
M8Z 5W9
Personal Care: skin, hair and bath care products; **Catalogue; Shop by Mail**

OLD GOLDENLAND
730 Thomas Avenue
St. Paul, Minnesota
55104
Personal Care

O'NATUREL INC.
2909 Park Boulevard
Oakland, California
94610
Personal Care: skin, hair and bath care products; **Catalogue; Shop by Mail**

ORIFLAME INTERNATIONAL
76 Treble Road
North Billerica, Maryland
01862
1599 Hurontario Street
Suite 101
Mississauga, Ontario
L5G 4S1
Cosmetics: colour make-up; **Personal Care:** skin, hair and bath care products; **Catalogue; Shop by Mail**

ORIENTAL BEAUTY SECRETS
1800 South Robertson Boulevard
Suite 182
Los Angeles, California
90035
Personal Care: skin and hair care products; **Catalogue; Shop by Mail**

ORJENE NATURAL COSMETICS
5-43 - 48th Avenue
Long Island City, New York
11101
Cosmetics: colour make-up; **Personal Care:** skin and hair care products; **Catalogue; Shop by Mail**

PAINLESSLY BEAUTIFUL
1260 Lumber Street
Middletown, Pennsylvania
17057
Cosmetics: colour make-up; **Personal Care:** skin and hair care products, men's toiletries; **Catalogue; Shop by Mail**

PANACEA
PO Box 294
Columbia, Pennsylvania
17512
Personal Care; Household Products; Catalogue; Shop by Mail

PATRICIA ALLISON
4470 Monahan Road
La Mesa, California
92041
Cosmetics: colour make-up; **Personal Care:** skin care products, perfumes; **Catalogue; Shop by Mail**

PAUL PENDERS USA
(c/o D&P Products)
PO Box 5601
2810 East Long Street
Tampa, Florida
33605-5601

(c/o Lifesource Limited)
91 Esna Park Drive
Markham, Ontario
L3R 2S2
Cosmetics: colour make-up; **Personal Care:** skin, hair and nail care products, bath care products, men's toiletries; **Catalogue; Shop by Mail**

PEACEFUL KINGDOM, THE
1902 West 6th Street South
Wilmington, Delaware
19805
Personal Care; Household Products; Catalogue; Shop by Mail

PETS 'N PEOPLE
5312 Ironwood Street
Rancho Palos Verdes, California
90274
Household Products; Pet Care Products; Catalogue; Shop by Mail

PROFESSIONAL & TECHNICAL SERVICES
3333 North East Sandy Boulevard
Number 208
Portland, Oregon
97232
Personal Care: skin care products; **Catalogue; Shop by Mail**

PURITAN'S PRIDE
105 Orville Drive
Bohemia, New York
11716
Cosmetics: colour make-up; **Personal Care:** skin, hair and body care products; **Catalogue; Shop by Mail**

QUEEN HELENE (PARA LABORATORIES, INC.)
100 Rose Avenue
Hempstead, New York
11550
Personal Care: bath care products; **Catalogue; Shop by Mail**

RACHEL PERRY
9111 Mason Avenue
Chatsworth, California
91311
Cosmetics: colour make-up; **Personal Care:** skin care products; **Catalogue**

RAINBOW RESEARCH CORPORATION
170 Wilbur Place
Bohemia, New York
11716
Personal Care: skin, hair and bath care products; **Catalogue; Shop by Mail**

W. T. RAWLEIGH COMPANY
223 East Main Street
Freeport, Illinois
61032
Personal Care: skin and hair care products; **Pet Care Products; Catalogue; Shop by Mail**

THE REAL ALOE COMPANY
4375 - 4D Industrial Street
Simi Valley, California
93063
Personal Care: skin, hair and bath care products; **Catalogue; Shop by Mail**

RED SAFFRON
3009 - 16th Avenue South
Minneapolis, Minnesota
55407
Personal Care: skin care products; **Household Products; Catalogue; Shop by Mail**

RENEE'S HAIRLINES
413 Capitola Avenue
Capitola, California
95010
Personal Care: hair care products

REVIVA LABS
705 Hopkins Road
Haddonfield, New Jersey
08033
Cosmetics: colour make-up; **Personal Care:** skin and hair care products; **Catalogue; Shop by Mail**

RHIZOTOME CO.
PO Box 588
Boulder, Colorado
80306
Personal Care: skin care products

RICHLIFE INC.
2211 East Orangewood
Anaheim, California
92806-0240

Personal Care: hair, baby care products; **Catalogue; Shop by Mail**

I. ROKEACH & SONS, INC.
560 Sylvan Avenue
Englewood, Cliffs, New Jersey
07632

Personal Care: bath care products; **Catalogue; Shop by Mail**

FRANK T. ROSS & SONS
6550 Lawrence Avenue East
West Hill, Ontario
M1E 4R5

Personal Care: hair care products; **Household Products; Catalogue; Shop by Mail**

RR INDUSTRIES
1612 West Olive
Number 301
Burbank, California
91506

Personal Care: skin care products; **Catalogue; Shop by Mail**

SAPPO HILL SOAPWORKS
654 Tolman Creek Road
Ashland, Oregon
97520

Personal Care: bath care products; **Catalogue; Shop by Mail**

SCHIFF
121 Moonachie Avenue
Moonachie, New Jersey
07074

Personal Care: skin and hair care products; **Catalogue; Shop by Mail**

SHAHIN SOAP COMPANY, THE
PO Box 2413
427 Van Dyke Avenue
Paterson, New Jersey
07509

Household Products; Catalogue; Shop by Mail

SHIKAI PRODUCTS
PO Box 2866
Santa Rosa, California
95405

Personal Care: hair care products; **Catalogue; Shop by Mail**

SHIRLEY PRICE AROMATHERAPY
462 - 62nd Street
Brooklyn, New York
11220

Personal Care: skin and bath care products; **Catalogue; Shop by Mail**

SIERRA DAWN BODY CARE
8687 Grafton Road
Sebastopol, California
95472

Personal Care: skin and bath care products; **Household Products; Catalogue; Shop by Mail**

SIRENA TROPIC SOAP
COMPANY
PO Box 31673
Dallas, Texas
75231
Personal Care: bath care products

SLEEPY HOLLOW
BOTANICALS
84 Galli Drive
Novato, California
94947
Personal Care: skin and hair care products; **Catalogue; Shop by Mail**

SOAPBERRY SHOP
50 Galaxy Blvd.
Rexdale, Ontario
M9W 4Y5
Cosmetics; Personal Care: body, hair, nail and bath care products; **Catalogue; Shop by Mail**

THE SOAP WORKS
60 Chatsworth Drive
Toronto, Ontario
M4R 1R5
Personal Care: bath care products; **Household Products**

SOLID GOLD HOLISTIC
ANIMAL EQUINE
NUTRITION CENTRE
1483 North Cuyumaca
El Cajon, California
92020
Personal Care

SOMBRA (C&S
LABORATORIES)
5600G McLeod Avenue
Albuquerque, New Mexico
87109
Cosmetics: colour make-up; **Personal Care:** skin and hair care products; **Catalogue; Shop by Mail**

STARWEST BOTANICAL, INC.
11253 Trade Centre Drive
Rancho Cordova, California
95670
Personal Care

ST. IVES INC.
944 Indian Peak Road
Rolling Hills, California
90274
Personal Care

SUNRISE LANE
780 Greenwich Street
Department DB
New York, New York
10014-2114
Cosmetics: colour make-up; **Personal Care:** skin, hair and bath care products; **Catalogue; Shop by Mail**

SUNSHINE SCENTED OILS
(SUNSHINE MARKETING
SERVICES)
1919 Burnside Avenue
Los Angeles, California
90016
Personal Care: skin care products, perfumes; **Catalogue; Shop by Mail**

TIKI (G. R. LANE HEALTH PRODUCTS LIMITED)
(c/o Donmar Health and Beauty Products)
210-A Denison Street
Markham, Ontario
L3R 1B6
Personal Care: skin and hair care products; **Catalogue; Shop by Mail**

T-LINE PRODUCTS
1501 East McMillan Street
Cincinnati, Ohio
45206
Cosmetics: colour make-up; **Personal Care; Household Products**

TOM'S OF MAINE
Railroad Avenue
Kennenbunk, Maine
04043
Personal Care: skin and hair care products; **Catalogue; Shop by Mail**

TRANS INDIA PRODUCTS
PO Box 2866
Santa Rosa, California
95405
Personal Care: hair care products; **Catalogue; Shop by Mail**

TROPICAL SOAP COMPANY
PO Box 31673
Dallas, Texas
75231
Personal Care: bath care products; **Catalogue; Shop by Mail**

UNI PAC LABORATORIES
6355 North Broadway
Chicago, Illinois
60660
Personal Care; Catalogue; Shop by Mail

VEGAN STREET
PO Box 5525
Rockville, Maryland
20855
Cosmetics: colour make-up; **Personal Care:** skin, hair and bath care products, perfumes, men's toiletries; **Household Products; Pet Care Products; Catalogue: Shop by Mail**

VELVET PRODUCTS
PO Box 5459
Beverly Hills, California
90209
Personal Care: skin care products, men's toiletries

VITABATH
(Vitabath is widely sold in drug stores and department stores in North America)
Personal Care: bath care products

VITAMIN QUOTA INC.
293 Madison Avenue
New York, New York
10017
Cosmetics: colour make-up

VIVIANE WOODWARD COSMETICS
7712 Densmore Avenue
Van Nuys, California
91406
Cosmetics: colour make-up

WALA-HEILMITTEL
(c/o Dr. Haushka Cosmetics
Incorporated)
GMBH, Meadowbrook West
Wyoming, Rhode Island
02898

Head Office:
D-7325 Eckwalden
West Germany
Personal Care: skin and bath care products; Catalogue; Shop by Mail

WARM EARTH COSMETICS
334 West 19th Street
Chico, California
95928
Cosmetics: colour make-up; Personal Care: skin care products; Catalogue; Shop by Mail

WEBBER INCORPORATED
3909 Nashua Drive
Mississauga, Ontario
L4V 1R3
Personal Care: skin and bath care products; Catalogue; Shop by Mail

WELEDA INCORPORATED
(c/o Michael Lange Enterprises)
PO Box 91817
West Vancouver, British Columbia
V7V 4S1

841 South Main Street
PO Box 769
Spring Valley, New York
10977
Personal Care: skin, hair and bath care products; Catalogue; Shop by Mail

WITHOUT HARM
4605 Pauli Drive
Manlius, New York
13104
Personal Care; Household Products; Catalogue; Shop by Mail

YES SOAP SHOP
1015 Wisconsin Avenue NW
Washington, District of Colombia
20007
Personal Care: bath care products

YOUTHESSENCE LIMITED
PO Box 3057
New York, New York
10185
Personal Care: skin care products; Catalogue; Shop by Mail

Chapter 6

CRUELTY-FREE COMPANIES IN THE UNITED KINGDOM

BARRY M
Unit 1, Bittacy Business Centre
Bittacy Hill
Mill Hill East, London
NW7 1BA

Cosmetics: colour make-up; **Personal Care:** skin, hair, nail and bath care products, men's toiletries; **Catalogue; Shop by Mail**

BEAUTY WITHOUT CRUELTY
37 Avery Avenue
Tonbridge, Kent
TN9 1TL

Cosmetics: colour make-up; **Personal Care:** skin, hair and nail care products, perfumes, men's toiletries; **Catalogue; Shop by Mail**

THE BODY SHOP INTERNATIONAL
Hawthorn Road, Wick
Littlehampton, West Sussex
BN1 77LR

Cosmetics: colour make-up; **Personal Care:** skin, hair, bath care products, perfumes, men's toiletries; **Catalogue; Shop by Mail**

(Over 80 shops located throughout the UK)

BODY CARE
50 High Street, Ide
Exeter, Devon
EX2 9RW

Personal Care: skin, bath care products; **Catalogue; Shop by Mail**

BODYLINE COSMETICS LTD.
Unit 5, Alders Way
Yalberton Industrial Estate
Paignton, Devon
TQ4 7QL
Personal Care: skin, hair, bath care products, perfumes, men's toiletries; Catalogue; Shop by Mail

CAMILLA HEPPER
Lion House
20-28 Muspole Street
Norwich, Norfolk
Personal Care: skin, hair, bath care products, perfumes, men's toiletries; Catalogue; Shop by Mail

CAURNIE SOAP COMPANY
The Soaperie, Canal Street
Kirkintilloch, Scotland
G66 1QZ
Personal Care: skin, hair, bath care products; Household Products; Catalogue; Shop by Mail

CHANDORE PERFUME
2 Ashtree Avenue
Mitcham, Surrey
Personal Care: perfumes; Catalogue; Shop by Mail

CHERISH COSMETICS
Jane Kendall
Western View, Sunny Bank
Great Longstone, Derbyshire
DE4 1TL
Cosmetics: colour make-up; Personal Care: skin care products

CREIGHTON PRODUCTS
Water Lane, Storrington
Pulborough, Sussex
RH20 3DP
Personal Care: skin, hair, bath care products; Catalogue; Shop by Mail

CRIMPERS PURE PRODUCTS
63-67 Heath Street
London
NW3 6UG
Personal Care: hair care products; Catalogue; Shop by Mail

CULPEPER LTD.
Hadstock Road
Linton, Cambridge
CB1 6NJ
Personal Care: skin, hair care products; Catalogue; Shop by Mail
(Shops located throughout the United Kingdom)

ECOVER
Charlton Court Farm
Mouse Lane
Steyning, West Sussex
BN4 3DF
Household Products

FAITH PRODUCTS
52-56 Albion Road
Edinburgh, Scotland
EH7 5QZ
Personal Care: skin, hair, bath care products; Catalogue; Shop by Mail

HENARA (HAIR HEALTH LTD.)
Classic House
174-180 Old Street
London
EC1
Personal Care: hair care products

HONESTY COSMETICS
33 Markham Road
Chesterfield, Derby
S40 1TA
Personal Care: skin, hair and bath care products, perfumes, men's toiletries; **Catalogue; Shop by Mail**

JANE HOWARD COSMETICS
The Cottage, 49 Springfield Street
Barnsley, South Yorkshire
Cosmetics; Personal Care

JANCO SALES
11 Seymour Road
Hampton Hill, Middlesex
TW12 1DD
Household Products

LEICHNER'S STAGE MAKE-UP
Beauty House
Hawthorne Road
Eastbourne, East Sussex
BN23 6QX
Personal Care: colour theatrical make-up

MANDALA AYURVEDIC IMPORTS
7 Zetland Road
Redland, Bristol
Personal Care; Catalogue; Shop by Mail

MARKS AND SPENCER
Michael House
Baker Street, London
W1A 1DN
Cosmetics: colour make-up; **Personal Care:** skin, hair, nail and body care products, men's toiletries
(Stores located throughout the UK)

MARTHA HILL
The Old Vicarage
Laxton, Northants
NN17 3BR
Cosmetics: colour make-up; **Personal Care:** skin, hair and bath care products, perfumes, men's toiletries; **Catalogue; Shop by Mail**

NATURAL BEAUTY PRODUCTS LTD.
Western Avenue
Bridgend Industrial Estate
Mid Glamorgan, Wales
CF31 3RT
Cosmetics: colour make-up; **Personal Care:** skin, hair and nail care products, perfumes, men's toiletries; **Catalogue; Shop by Mail**

NUTRI-METICS INTERNATIONAL
15 Erica Road
Stacey Bushes
Milton Keynes, Bucks
Cosmetics: colour make-up; **Personal Care:** skin, hair, nail and bath care products, perfumes, men's toiletries; **Household Products; Catalogue; Shop by Mail**

PECKSNIFES
45-46 Meeting House Lane
Brighton, Sussex
Personal Care: skin, hair and bath care products, perfumes; **Catalogue; Shop by Mail**

PURE PLANT PRODUCTS
42 Sandy Lane
Irby
Wirral, Merseyside
L47 3BS
Personal Care: skin, hair and bath care products, perfumes; **Catalogue; Shop by Mail**

QUEEN COSMETICS
130 Wigmore Street
London
W1H 0AT
Personal Care: skin and hair care products

REFORM COSMETICS
The House of Regency
5 Kingsway Buildings
Bridgent Industrial, Bridgent
Mid Glamorgan, Wales
CF31 3SD
(shops throughout the United Kingdom)
Cosmetics: colour make-up; **Personal Care:** skin, hair and nail care products, perfumes, men's toiletries

RITA SHAW
3 Juniper Court
26 College Hill Road
Harrow Weald, Middlesex
HA3 7H3
Personal Care: skin care products

SARAKAN LTD.
106 High Street
Beckenham, Kent
BR3 1EB

SHIRLEY PRICE AROMATH-ERAPY LTD.
Wesley House
Stockwell Head
Hinckley, Leicester
LE10 1RD
Personal Care; Catalogue; Shop by Mail

SIMPLY HERBAL
Kingsway
Murdock
Wilton, Wiltshire
SP2 0AW
Personal Care: skin and hair care products; **Catalogue; Shop by Mail**

TIKI COSMETICS (UK)
Sisson Road
Gloucester, Gloucestershire
GL1 3QB
Personal Care: skin, hair, bath care products; **Catalogue; Shop by Mail**

WELEDA (UK)
Heanor House
Ilkeston, Derbyshire
Personal Care: skin, hair and bath care products; **Catalogue; Shop by Mail**

WINSTON
Illingworth Health Foods
York House, York Street
Bradford
Personal Care: skin and bath care products

YING YANG BEAUTY CARE
Abbey Chase
Bridge Road
Chertsey, Surrey
United Kingdom
Personal Care: skin care products; **Catalogue; Shop by Mail**

Chapter 7

ANIMAL WELFARE GROUPS IN CANADA AND THE UNITED STATES

ACTION VOLUNTEERS FOR ANIMALS (AVA)
3 Brookfield Road
Willowdale,Ontario
M2P 1B1

- promotes all aspects of animal issues and the prevention of cruelty
- active in increasing public awareness of animal protection and humane treatment, through literature and newsletters
- membership

ALBERTANS FOR THE ETHICAL TREATMENT OF ANIMALS (AETA)
PO Box 3734, Station D
Edmonton, Alberta
T5L 4J7

- promotes all aspects of animal issues and the prevention of cruelty
- active in increasing public awareness of animal protection and humane treatment, through literature and newsletter

THE AMERICAN ANTI-VIVISECTION SOCIETY
801 Old York Road
Suite 204, Noble Plaza
Jenkintown, Pennsylvania
19046-1685

- promotes all aspects of animal issues and the prevention of cruelty
- active to abolish all experiments of live animals
- newsletter and educational packs
- membership

AMERICAN FUND FOR ALTERNATIVES TO ANIMAL RESEARCH
175 West 12th Street, Suite 16G
New York, New York
10011-8275
- sponsors research projects for alternatives to live animals
- active in increasing public awareness of animal research and alternatives, through educational packs
- membership

THE AMERICAN SOCIETY FOR THE PREVENTION OF CRUELTY TO ANIMALS (ASPCA)
441 East 92nd Street
New York, New York
10128
- promotes all aspects of animal issues and the prevention of cruelty
- active to abolish experiments of live animals, as well as animal trapping and ranching for furs
- newsletter and education packs
- membership

THE AMERICAL VEGAN SOCIETY
501 Old Harding Highway
Malaga, New Jersey
08328
- active in increasing public awareness of animal research and alternatives
- newsletter and educational packs
- membership

THE ANIMAL'S CRUSADERS
1402 Larch Street
Everett, Washington
98201
- promotes all aspects of animal issues and the prevention of cruelty
- newsletter and educational packs
- membership

ANIMAL DEFENCE LEAGUE OF CANADA
PO Box 3880, Station C
Ottawa, Ontario
K1Y 4M5
- promotes all aspects of animal issues, especially trapping and laboratory experiments
- information packs
- membership

ANIMAL RIGHTS CONNECTION
PO Box 9023
Berkeley, California
94709
- promotes all aspects of animal issues, especially the abolishment of trapping and laboratory experiments
- information packs
- membership

ARK II USA
PO Box 11049
Washington, District of Columbia
20008
- promotes all aspects of animal issues and the prevention of cruelty

84

- especially concerned with increasing public awareness of live animal experiments and wildlife trapping for furs
- information packs
- membership

ASSOCIATION OF VETERINARIANS FOR ANIMAL RIGHTS (AVAR)
530 East Putnam Avenue
Greenwich, Connecticut
06830

- mandate to seek the prevention of live animal experiments
- active in promoting public awareness and humane treatment of animals through literature and information packs
- membership

BEAUTY WITHOUT CRUELTY
175 West 12th Street
New York, New York
10011
(not affiliated with the cosmetic company of the same name)

- promotes a cruelty-free lifestyle
- active to abolish animal testing of cosmetics and household products
- newsletter, information pack, and list of cruelty-free contacts for the US
- membership

CANADIAN VEGANS FOR ANIMAL RIGHTS (C-VAR)
c/o General Delivery
Port Perry, Ontario
L0B 1N0

- promotes all aspects of animal issues and the prevention of cruelty
- especially concerned with biomedical research, factory farming and live animal testing
- literature, newsletter and information packs
- membership

COALITION TO ABOLISH THE LD50 AND DRAIZE TESTS
PO Box 214, Planetarium Station
New York, New York
10024

- active to abolish the LD50 and Draize tests, and concerned with increasing public awareness on live animal testing
- information pack and newsletter
- membership

COALITION TO END ANIMAL SUFFERING AND EXPLOITATION (CEASE)
PO Box 27
Cambridge, Massachusetts
02238

- promotes all aspects of animal issues and the prevention of cruelty
- information packs and newsletter
- membership

CONCORDIA ANIMAL RIGHTS ASSOCIATION
PO Box 35
Outremont, Quebec
H2V 4M6

- promotes all aspects of animal issues and the prevention of cruelty
- newsletter and information packs
- membership

CULTURE AND ANIMAL FOUNDATION
3509 Eden Croft Drive
Raleigh, North Carolina
27612

- promotes all aspects of animal issues and the prevention of cruelty
- newsletter and information packs
- membership

DORIS DAY ANIMAL LEAGUE
111 Massachusetts Avenue North West, Suite 200
Washington, District of Columbia
20001

- promotes all aspects of animal issues, especially the abolishment of trapping and ranching animals for furs
- information packs and newsletter
- membership

FASHION WITH COMPASSION
PO Box 303
Burton, Washington
98013

- promotes a cruelty-free lifestyle
- especially concerned with research on live animals, and trapping and ranching for furs
- information packs

FOCUS ON ANIMALS
PO Box 150
Trumbull, Connecticut
06611

- promotes all aspects of animal issues and the prevention of cruelty
- information pack and newsletter
- membership

FRIENDS OF ANIMALS
Administrative Office
1 Pine Street
Neptune, New Jersey
07753

- promotes all aspects of animal issues and the prevention of cruelty
- active in increasing public awareness of animal protection and humane treatment, through literature and newsletters
- membership

86

THE FUND FOR ANIMALS
200 West 57th Street
New York , New York
10019

- promotes all aspects of animal issues and the prevention of cruelty
- information packs and newsletter
- membership

GREENPEACE
240 Fort Mason
San Francisco, California
94123

578 Bloor Street West
Toronto, Ontario
M6G 9Z9

- promotes all aspects of animal and environmental issues, such as endangered wildlife and marine life species
- information packs and newsletter
- membership

THE HUMANE SOCIETY OF THE UNITED STATES
2100 L Street, NW
Washington, District of Columbia
20037

- promotes all aspects of animal issues and the prevention of cruelty
- active in increasing public awareness of animal research and alternatives, through educational packs
- membership

IN DEFENCE OF ANIMALS
21 Tamal Vista Boulevard
Corte Madera, California
94925

- promotes all aspects of animal issues and the prevention of cruelty
- newsletter and information packs
- membership

INTERNATIONAL FOUNDATION FOR ETHICAL RESEARCH
79 West Monroe, Suite 514
Chicago, Illinois
60603

- promotes and sponsors research of alternatives to animal testing
- newsletter and information pack
- membership

INTERNATIONAL FUND FOR ANIMAL WELFARE (IFAW)
PO Box 193
Yarmouth Port, Massachusetts
02675

150 Bridgeland Avenue, Suite 207
Toronto, Ontario
M6A 1Z5

- promotes all aspects of animal and environmental issues
- active in increasing public awareness of animal and environmental protection through literature and newsletters
- information pack
- membership

INTERNATIONAL SOCIETY FOR ANIMAL RIGHTS, INC.
421 South State Street
Clarks Summit, Pennsylvania
18411

- promotes all aspects of animal issues and the prevention of cruelty
- newsletter, and information packs
- membership

LIFEFORCE FOUNDATION
PO Box 3117
Main Post Office
Vancouver, British Columbia
V6B 3X6

Box 825
North Hollywood, California
91603

Box 210354
San Francisco, California
94121

- promotes all aspects of animal and environmental issues, such as endangered wildlife and marine life species; especially active to abolish the seal hunt
- information packs and newsletter
- membership

MANITOBA ANIMAL RIGHTS COALITION
255 Montgomery Avenue
Winnipeg, Manitoba
R3L 1T3

- promotes all aspects of animal issues and the prevention of cruelty
- newsletter
- membership

MARYLAND LEGISLATION FOR ANIMAL WELFARE
PO Box 9110
Silver Spring, Maryland
20906

- active to abolish the Draize and LD50 for cosmetics and household products in the state of Maryland

MOBILIZATION FOR ANIMALS
PO Box 1679
Columbus, Ohio
43216

- promotes all aspects of animal issues and the prevention of cruelty
- newsletter and information packs
- membership

THE NATIONAL ANTI-VIVISECTION SOCIETY (NAVS)
100 East Ohio Street
Chicago, Illinois
60611

- active to abolish all tests on live animals
- active in increasing public awareness of vivisection and alternatives, through newsletter and educational packs
- membership

THE NEW ENGLAND ANTI-VIVISECTION SOCIETY
333 Washington Street, Suite 850
Boston, Massachusetts
02108

- active to abolish all tests on live animals
- active in increasing public awareness of vivisection and alternatives, through newsletter and educational packs
- membership

PEOPLE FOR THE ETHICAL TREATMENT OF ANIMALS (PETA)
PO Box 42516
Washington, District of Columbia
20015

- promotes all aspects of animal issues and the prevention of cruelty
- active to abolish all experiments on live animals, especially in the cosmetic and household product industry
- newsletter and information packs
- membership

PHYSICIAN'S COMMITTEE FOR RESPONSIBLE MEDICINE
PO Box 6322
Washington, District of Columbia
20015

- active to abolish all tests on live animals and to promote alternatives, from a "professional" point of view

- newsletter
- membership

PROGRESSIVE ANIMAL WELFARE SOCIETY (PAWS)
15305 - 44th Avenue West
PO Box 1037
Lynnwood, Washington
98036

- especially active in the prevention of trapping, and ranching for furs
- active in increasing public awareness of animal research and alternatives, through newsletter and information packs
- membership

SOCIETY FOR ANIMAL PROTECTIVE LEGISLATION
PO Box 3719
Georgetown Station
Washington, District of Columbia
20007

- promotes all aspects of animal issues and the prevention of cruelty
- newsletter and information packs
- membership

STUDENTS FOR THE ETHICAL TREATMENT OF ANIMALS (SETA)
112 Arbour Glenn, Suite 910
London, Ontario
N5Y 2A2

- students promoting all aspects of animal issues and the prevention of cruelty
- newsletter

SUPPRESS
750 East Bolorado Boul., Suite 6
Pasadena, California
91101

- promotes all aspects of animal issues and the prevention of cruelty
- newsletter and information packs
- membership

THE TORONTO HUMANE SOCIETY (THS)
11 River Street
Toronto, Ontario
M5A 4C2

- promotes all aspects of animal issues and the prevention of cruelty; active to abolish all tests on live animals, especially in the cosmetic and household products industry
- newsletter and information packs
- membership

TRANS-SPECIES UNLIMITED
PO Box 1553
Williamsport, Pennsylvania
17703

- promotes all aspects of animal issues and the prevention of cruelty
- newsletter and information packs
- membership

UNITED ACTION FOR ANIMALS, INC.
205 East 42nd Street
New York, New York
10017

- promotes all aspects of animal issues and the prevention of cruelty
- newsletter and information packs
- membership

WORLD SOCIETY FOR THE PROTECTION OF ANIMALS
PO Box 190
29 Perkins Street
Boston, Massachusetts
02130

215 Lakeshore Blvd. E., Suite 113
Toronto, Ontario
M5A 3W9

- promotes all aspects of animal and environmental issues
- newsletter and information packs
- membership

Chapter 8

ANIMAL WELFARE GROUPS IN THE UNITED KINGDOM

ANIMAL AID
111 High Street
Tonbridge, Kent
TN9 1BH

- active to abolish all tests on live animals, especially in the cosmetics and household product industry
- newsletter and information packs
- membership

ANIMAL CONCERN
121 West Regent Street
Glasgow, Scotland
G2 2SD

- promotes all aspects of animal issues and the prevention of cruelty
- newsletter

BRITISH UNION FOR THE ABOLITION OF VIVISECTION (BUAV)
16-A Crane Grove
London
N78 LB

- active to abolish all experiments on live animals, especially in the cosmetics and household product industry
- newsletter and information packs
- membership

DERBY AND BURTON ANIMAL WELFARE
37 Hathern Close
Sunnyhill, Derby
DE3 7NE

- promotes all aspects of animal issues and the prevention of cruelty
- newsletter
- membership

FIGHT ANIMAL CRUELTY EVERYWHERE (FACE)
Danbury View
Peverel Avenue, Nounsley
Hatfield Peverel (near Chelmsford),
Essex
CM3 2NA

- promotes all aspects of animal issues and the prevention of cruelty
- information packs
- membership

FUND FOR THE REPLACEMENT OF ANIMALS IN MEDICAL EXPERIMENTS (FRAME)
Eastgate House
34 Stoney Street,
Nottingham
NG1 1NB

- promotes research of alternatives to live animals tests; especially active to abolish all experiments on live animals
- newsletter and information packs
- membership

GREENPEACE
36 Graham Street
London
N18 LL

- promotes all aspects of animal and environmental issues, such as endangered wildlife and marine life species
- information packs and newsletter
- membership

HARBOROUGH ANIMAL CONCERN
22 Brookfield Road
Market Harborough, Leicester
LE1 69DU

- promotes all aspects of animal issues and the prevention of cruelty
- newsletter

INTERNATIONAL ASSOCIATION AGAINST PAINFUL EXPERIMENTS ON ANIMALS (IAAPEA)
PO Box 215
St. Albans, Hertfordshire
AL3 4RD

- active to abolish all experiments on live animals
- newsletter
- membership

INTERNATIONAL FUND FOR ANIMAL WELFARE (IFAW)
Tubwell House, New Road
Crowborough, East Sussex
TN5 2MQ

- promotes all aspects of animal issues, and the prevention of cruelty
- newsletter and information packs
- membership

THE NATIONAL ANTI-VIVISECTION SOCIETY
51 Harley Street
London
W1N 1DD

- active to abolish all tests on live animals

- active in increasing public awareness of vivisection and alternatives, through newsletter and educational packs
- membership

ROYAL SOCIETY FOR THE PREVENTION OF CRUELTY TO ANIMALS (RSPCA)
The Causeway
Horsham, West Sussex
RH12 1HG

- promotes all aspects of animal issues and the prevention of cruelty
- newsletter and information packs
- membership

THE SCOTTISH SOCIETY FOR THE PREVENTION OF VIVISECTION
10 Queensferry Street
Edinburgh, Scotland
EH2 4PG

- active to abolish all experiments on live animals
- newsletter and information packs
- membership

THE VEGAN SOCIETY
33-35 George Street
Oxford
OX1 2AY

- promotes a cruelty-free lifestyle, all aspects of animal issues and the prevention of cruelty
- newsletter and information packs
- membership

WORLD ANIMAL WELFARE GROUP
8 Paslowes, Vange
Basildon, Essex
SS16 4LS

- promotes all aspects of animal issues and the prevention of cruelty
- newsletter and information packs
- membership

WORLD SOCIETY FOR THE PROTECTION OF ANIMALS (WSPA)
106 Jeremy Street
London
SW1Y 6EE

- promotes all aspects of animal and environmental issues
- newsletter
- membership

93

OTHER BOOKS OF INTEREST TO ANIMAL LOVERS FROM SUMMERHILL PRESS*

Emergency Care for Cats and Dogs
First Aid for Your Pet
Craton Burkholder, D.V.M., M.A.

Unless you have a resident vet, you'll need *Emergency Care for Cats and Dogs* to help you make the right decisions concerning the needs of your pets. This well organized and straightforward guide provides pointers on diagnosing and treating ailments, what to do if your pet is injured and everyday care such as feeding and grooming. Common catastrophes such as skunk odour and porcupine quills can be easily solved with the aid of this book.

...should be in every home where there is a cat or dog.
DR. MICHAEL W. FOX,
SCIENTIFIC DIRECTOR OF THE HUMANE SOCIETY
OF THE UNITED STATES

Care of the Wild, Feathered and Furred
Treating and Feeding Injured Birds and Animals
Mae Hickman and Maxine Guy

Next time you encounter an injured wild bird or animal, you'll know how to care for it with the help of this book. This attractive volume tells you how to raise baby birds and animals, splint broken bones, remove tar and oil, treat poisoning, shock and a variety of other diseases and disabilities.

...quite simply the most complete and authoritative handbook on the treatment and feeding of injured birds and animals available today. This is a 'must have' volume for everyone with an interest in wildlife.
BOOKS NOW

* These titles published by Michael Kesend Publishing, Ltd. in the United States